LISTEN

TO THE

DESERT

LISTEN
TO THE
DESERT

SECRETS OF SPIRITUAL MATURITY FROM THE DESERT FATHERS AND MOTHERS

GREGORY MAYERS

TRIUMPH™ BOOKS
Liguori, Missouri

Published by Triumph™ Books
Liguori, Missouri
An Imprint of Liguori Publications

Imprimi Potest
Very Reverend Monroe G. Perrier, C.Ss.R.
Vice Provincial Superior
New Orleans Vice Province
The Redemptorists
July 1, 1996

Imprimatur
Msgr. James C. Gurzynski, JCL
Vicar General, Diocese of Amarillo
Amarillo, Texas
July 19, 1996

Library of Congress Cataloging-in-Publication Data

Mayers, Gregory.
   Listen to the desert : secrets of spiritual maturity from the Desert Fathers and Mothers / Gregory Mayers—1st ed.
      p. cm.
   Includes bibliographical references.
   ISBN 0-89243-930-0
   1. Desert Fathers. 2. Spiritual life—Christianity—History of doctrines—Early church, ca. 30-600. I. Title.
BR195.C5M38 1996
248.4'811—dc20   96-12888

CONTENTS

FOREWORD

When I set out to write this book, I intended it to be a clear explanation of the spiritual journey for the typical educated reader. I chose this goal for two reasons. First, I'm not capable of a scholarly work, most of which, at any rate, seem to be inaccessible except to other scholars. Second, what has traditionally been labeled "mysticism" and as such reserved for the rare "worthy" individual is, in reality, the common heritage and full flowering of Christianity, and therefore ought to be accessible to all of us.

My intention was to use common experiences—experiences that any individual could assent to, could say of, "Yes, that's something I experience"—as a way of leading into an explanation of the zigzag path of spiritual maturity. All of this I hoped to do in fresh language, avoiding as much as possible the stilted vocabulary of ascetical and mystical theology and contemporary religious jargon, which seems to have been hijacked into the service of narrow ideologies, confused psychobabble, and justifications for dangerous religious enthusiasm.

Now that I've completed the work, I must admit to the horrible sense that all I've done is to scratch the surface of the task I set for myself. Whether I have, at least partially, accomplished my goal, I leave to the judgment of you, the reader. Parenthetically, and by way of analogy, I have a greater appreciation for the numerous disclaimers I hear regularly from parents who feel they've hardly done enough in raising their children.

Many people deserve, and have, my heartfelt gratitude for their help in preparing this book. First of all, my teacher, Father Willigis Jäger, OSB, who with patience that appears to me to be heroic at times and providential wisdom, continues to guide me on my own spiritual journey, as he has done for some fifteen years now. I couldn't possess whatever clarity I may enjoy in this subject without him. I am also indebted to Mrs. Joan Reich, Rev. James Chaumont, Mrs. Grace Mojtabai, and Mrs. Lorette Zirker, who corrected my glaring mistakes and offered invaluable suggestions to make the initial manuscript readable. I am deeply grateful for the considerable amount of time and the attention to detail that each of them dedicated to the task. Very special recognition goes to Mr. Bob Walker. Only he knows the significance of his assistance in preparing the manuscript for publication. Finally I am indebted to the many, many people I've met along the way who continue to be devoted to the spiritual life. Some I am privileged to live with, my Redemptorist confreres. Others, lay men and lay women (many are anonymous to me), have been an inspiration during the longer contemplative retreats we shared together in silence. All have given me by quiet example the conviction that it matters how an individual lives his or her life, especially in things deemed trivial. Each person, although I am sure these individuals are unaware of it, has contributed not only to my personal spiritual quest but also to the evolution of consciousness.

GREGORY MAYERS, C.Ss.R.
Amarillo, Texas
APRIL 1996

Dedicated to:

My father
who taught me by example
the secret of love and life

PREFACE

S tudent turned teacher. That was one of my main thoughts as I read the manuscript of this book of Father Gregory Mayers. My thoughts went back to the early 1960s, when I taught Greg in our Redemptorist high school seminary, and now I found myself being masterfully taught by my student. As his former spiritual director, I was proud to be reading a work that was evidently the product of a deep spirituality.

Father Mayers digs into early Christian roots and reveals a spirituality that has meaning for our day. What has traditionally been labeled mysticism and claimed to be reserved for the rare worthy individual he shows to be the common heritage and full flowering of Christianity, which should be accessible to all. This book proceeds from many years of experience in his own spiritual journey. His words come freely, and his thoughts flow from a spiritual maturity and a practice that is now natural to him.

The rewards for you who read this book will be great, especially if you follow this suggestion. Although the words and thoughts are clear, they should be read with determination and great concentration. There are concepts in this book that are so fresh they need to be nourished with silence and reflection in order to grasp what follows.

This is not a how-to manual on the spiritual life. However, Father Mayers explains and encourages a practice that is most helpful and could lead to a spiritual path not previously dreamed of. Do the book justice: Do yourself a favor and take the time to do the practice.

VERY REVEREND MONROE G. PERRIER, C.SS.R.
NEW ORLEANS, LOUISIANA
JULY 1, 1996

INTRODUCTION

Within a few hundred years after the birth of Christ, the thirst for a deepening life of prayer and faith was felt in the deserts of northern Africa. This thirst gave rise to the beginnings of Christian contemplative practice, which flourished in the regions along the Nile. These early beginnings of monastic life attracted many from Egypt, as well as from other parts of the ancient world, and inspired similar monastic foundations throughout the Mediterranean region, spreading eventually to Europe and beyond.

The initial inspiration for this desert monastic movement is largely attributed to Saint Antony of Egypt. Antony was born around the year 250. When he was about eighteen years old, both his parents died, leaving him suddenly with the responsibility of looking after a household. Burdened by these new concerns, he pondered the gospel passage, "Sell all you have and give to the poor." These words pierced his heart: Unable to ignore them, he soon divested the considerable family inheritance and distributed his money and goods among the poor. For the next fifteen years he inquired into the practices of various hermits and ascetics scattered about the region. While striving to advance in the spiritual life, Antony continued to live near his own hometown, taking on manual work to provide for his needs and giving what excess he had to the poor.

Although he remained dedicated to a life of poverty, self-sacrifice, and discipline, and his reputation had grown considerably, Antony continued to strive for a more complete abandonment to the life of faith and prayer. At about age thirty-five he began pressing deeper into remote places. He stayed for a time locked away in a tomb, where a friend would bring him supplies he needed for daily sustenance. Here he soon encountered temptations of a most egregious nature that, at one point, left him physically tormented, beaten, and all but lifeless. When the friend who had been tending to him found him unconscious in the tomb, he carried Antony to a church, where the local people gathered around for a vigil watch. Stirring back to consciousness in the middle of the night, Antony found himself surrounded by a group of sleeping people. Only his friend had remained awake at his side, and Antony begged to be carried back and locked once again in the tomb, where he could resume his trials. Unable to stand up for prayer, he lay in a state of helplessness as the tomb was shaken by visions of wild animals. Lions and bulls, snakes and scorpions, all appeared before Antony, assaulting him physically, but he remained calm and called out to his adversaries, "If there were some power among you, it would have been enough for only one of you to come."

Soon after this, the building in which the tomb was housed, which had been shaken from its foundations, became once again intact. The demons and beasts retreated in confusion and disappeared, the pain immediately left his body, the roof opened, and the tomb was filled with light. Aware of the vision, Antony felt his breathing grow steady, and he asked, "Where were you? Why didn't you appear in the beginning, so that you could stop my distresses?" And a voice came to him: "I was here, Antony, but I waited to watch your struggle. And now, since you persevered and were not defeated, I will be your helper forever."[1]

After this Antony pressed even deeper into the wilderness. He sealed himself in an old fort for many years, living mostly on dried loaves of bread and water. He had little contact with others, but still his reputation grew, and many followers began to congregate in the vicinity of the fort. At last these followers became impatient for instruction and tore off the fortress doors. After many years of seclusion Antony, quite fit, healthy, and radiant, emerged to an admiring throng.

During a brief public life Antony performed healings, settled disputes, consoled the troubled, delivered sermons, and inspired many others to take up the solitary life. Little by little the mountains and the deserts of the surrounding regions were peopled by those eager to emulate Antony and live a disciplined life of prayer and contemplation. But soon enough he again withdrew deeper into the wilderness. Escorted by a band of nomadic travelers, he went to an inner mountain, where he found a spring of perfectly clear water and a few date palms. He fell in love with this place, and in time he located a plot of ground nearby that was suitable for plowing. He planted wheat for flour so that he could provide for his own needs and those of his occasional guests. What he had in excess he sent back with travelers to the poor of the cities. Antony lived out his days on this inner mountain, sometimes leaving the place to assist the gatherings of monks that were forming in the area, sometimes providing for visitors, but always faithful to the solitary life of prayer and discipline until, in the year 356, he died at the age of 105.

Within less than forty years of Antony's death, monastic life had begun to spread throughout the Mediterranean region. Sometime in the year 394 seven monks set out from their own monastery in Jerusalem and traveled to visit Egypt. One of the first monks they visited, John of Lycopolis, warmly received them and, heartened by their determination to travel such a distance to a remote and difficult region, asked, "And what remarkable thing did you expect to find, my dearest children, that you have undertaken such a long journey with so much labour in your desire to visit some poor simple men who possess nothing worth seeing or admiring? Those who are worthy of admiration and praise are everywhere: the apostles and prophets of God, who are read in the churches. They are the ones you must imitate. I marvel at your zeal, how taking no account of so many dangers you have come to us to be edified, while we from laziness do not even wish to come out of our caves."[2]

But far from disappointed by these "poor and simple

men," the travelers continued on their tour. They recorded just a few of the encounters they had with the desert monks, but they were astounded to witness thousands, even tens of thousands, of nuns and monks living in the areas they visited. And although one modern writer points out that if their estimates of the populations of monks and nuns were tallied together, it would exceed the entire known population of the country of Egypt at that time,[3] we can nevertheless assume that this way of life, largely unheard of before Antony, had, in a very short time, become enormously popular.

By the time these seven traveled to the deserts, the practices of the Egyptian monastic settlements varied widely and were roughly divided into three styles. Some of the monks, following the inspiration of Saint Antony, remained deep in the deserts living eremetical lives, sometimes inhabiting caves or cliffs, sometimes wandering from place to place as itinerant hermits carrying on with their own peculiar practices and having little contact with others. There were also large groups who, under the inspiration of Saint Pachomius, lived together with others in enclosed monasteries and provided for all their needs without ever venturing outside the walls of their enclosure.

During their travels, the monks from Jerusalem visited the monastery of Isidore but were not able to enter. This was the most extreme of the enclosures, and their only contact was with the gatekeeper, an elderly monk who explained that only those who want to remain inside the walls of the monastery for the rest of their lives are allowed to enter, and once they enter, they never again leave the place.[4] Still other groups of monks had gathered around the teachings and guidance of a single master who had gained a reputation as a gifted spiritual director. These monks built small huts or cells consisting of one or two very simple rooms built hastily from crude bricks and mud. Upon approaching one such gathering of monks not far from Nitria, the monks from Jerusalem found that "they inhabit a desert place and have their cells some distance from each other, so that no one should be recognised from afar by another, or be seen easily, or hear another's voice. On the contrary, they live in profound silence, each monk isolated on his own. They come together in the churches only on Saturdays and Sundays, and meet one another."[5]

Much of what we know of these early foundations of the Christian contemplative life come from recorded accounts of outsiders like the ones cited above. These secondhand accounts, such as *The Life of Antony* written by Athanasius, bishop of Alexandria, and *Historia Monachorum in AEgypt*, written by one of the seven monks from Jerusalem, circulated widely in the ancient world and were popular and influential. Athanasius knew Antony personally, and his account, written with much passion, has all the elements of a good story. Following along from beginning to end, the reader sees Antony, in the fashion of a mythic hero, set out from his home, encounter many difficulties, pass through an experience of death and resurrection, defeat his enemies, hold to his ideals steadfastly, and set the world aright by his radiant presence. The account in *Historia Monachorum in AEgypt* is shaped like a travel journal and has all the wide-eyed naiveté and attention to the novelties of individual encounters with foreign people and places, all the dangers of traveling in strange and hostile regions, that make this genre so enjoyable to read even in our own day.

But when we turn to the direct accounts of the life of the desert gathered by the monks themselves, we encounter something altogether strange and foreign. These writings are collections of brief, loosely connected passages that range in length from a few sentences to a page or two. The stories and sayings were gathered by the monks, who circulated these writings among themselves for their own purposes. In these collections, though much can be inferred, we find little direct record or artfully arranged accounts of the sort of life that the monks led. We find no programs for spiritual advancement, no body of doctrine, no specific rules of conduct. When first turning to these writings the reader might be disappointed, for there is little that stimulates the intellect and imagination, inspires the spirit, or edifies the soul. The sayings of the old men give us a glimpse into a hard life, lived close to the desert floor in heat and cold. These stories and sayings were no doubt quite instructive to the ancients who shared that life and to those who have striven to emulate it since, but they can seem more than a little eccentric by modern standards.

However, as we take up these stories, one by one, it is possible to discover that, driven more by appetite than by hunger, we have grown used to going to our kitchens absent-mindedly, expecting to find a loaf of bread. By opening these writings, we feel as if we have come to a cupboard where we are now faced with only a bag of flour, a box of salt, and a package of yeast, and have no sure ideas about how to transform these into something that will feed our growing hunger. But herein lies the peculiar power of these writings to place us face to face with the old monks. It is the time we spend with the ingredients—the mixing, the rising, the baking, the buttering—it is the time we spend, before sinking our teeth past the warm crust, that places us in closer contact with the ancient world and allows the strangeness of that world to shape itself, gain texture, and grow increasingly familiar. In these sayings of the old monks, we are slowed down by the raw stuff of the contemplative life, and as we ourselves return again and again to the practice of contemplation, the odd and difficult experiences of the monks recorded in these stories become more and more recognizable, and it grows easier to understand a story like this one:

> A certain old man was deeply disturbed by thoughts for ten years, so much so that he was very hopeless, saying: My spirit is a wreck; and as long as I have perished once and for all, I shall return to the world. However when he was setting out, a voice came to him, saying: The ten years in which you have struggled, they are your crown. So return to your place, and I will liberate you from all troublesome thoughts. And immediately returning, he again took up the basic work of contemplation. Therefore it is not good to grow hopeless in any way on account of your thoughts. These truly provide for us a great crown, if, taking advantage, we pass through them with careful attention.[6]

Many of us might find it difficult to imagine ourselves being locked up in a tomb and enduring hordes of ravaging beasts as Saint Antony did. But anyone who has tried, even for ten minutes, to still the mind and quiet the thoughts can appreciate the hardships of this monk. And as with this old monk, as we take up the practice of contemplation, no matter how mundane and fruitless it might seem, bit by bit our life too is transformed. The ego may be slow to give up its grip on what it sees as its central position of control, but much good work goes on out of the immediate sight of our active mind. Our steady efforts accumulate slowly and settle out of sight. Then, suddenly, quite often during one of those times when the ego has begun to lose its grip and is ready to give up its efforts, those things that once seemed to hinder the practice of contemplation now appear as the very fruits of our steady effort. The practice and the way we must follow become clear and obvious, and the doubts that have prompted us to continue on our way disappear. And when we come to see with an eye that is whole and single and steady, we simply go on with this basic work of contemplation, although now with greater ease and confidence, fully aware that the union we have been seeking was a fact of our life long before we began our search.

It is just this beginning that Saint Antony discovered while locked in the tomb. He had stayed close to his home for a long time, studying to advance in virtue, discipline, and prayer, gathering advice and experience, and putting these into practice. Only after long, dedicated attention did he realize, in a moment of awakening, that all those things that were assaulting him, all the beasts and demons that were binding and piercing him, were always completely impotent and powerless against the truth of his existence.

Only then did he notice that the roof that sealed him in the tomb was porous and transparent. Only then did he realize that the room was filled with an ever-present light. The thirst that began to stir in Saint Antony—and also in the monk who nearly gave up after ten years of desert life—was a thirst for the presence, the certainty, and the peace of just this light.

The practice that Antony inspired was free to form and adapt itself accordingly in each new situation. Just as in his own day variant approaches arose that satisfied the thirst for prayer and contemplation, today there are many approaches to individuals' own contemplative practice. What remains constant, though, are our individual responsibilities—of jobs and studies, alongside family and friends, in the midst of disputes and misunderstandings, and other situations both difficult and rewarding. Such contemplative practice, although much different in appearance, is no less vital than the practice of those early desert monks and nuns. Our efforts might seem ineffective, and they might seem to disappear amid of the routines of our daily life, but this is as it should be. The salt hiding in the soup makes it tasty. The yeast in the dough turns it into bread. The more hidden the practice becomes in our daily life, the more it disappears to where it can do its work. And, as is so apparent with Saint Antony, much good is attracted to the presence of silence and stillness, and much is set in motion by diligent attention to what is closest to our hearts.

In *Listen to the Desert* Father Mayers has made a few of the most appropriately ripe desert sayings accessible to the modern reader. Drawing on his many years of experience as contemplative teacher and spiritual director, he offers a simple, practical approach, which is grounded by his own years of practice and clarified with a wealth of insights gained from a careful study of transpersonal psychology. Following the simple instructions found in *Listen to the Desert*, the reader can establish and maintain a regular contemplative practice. This book will be a great help not only for the beginner, but for everyone seeking to advance in the contemplative life for, again and again, the author makes it clear that there is no advance. There is only, always was only, and will forever be only, this unitive experience of ultimate truth that we are best encouraged to uncover by simply not covering it over.

Bob Walker
Jekyll Island, Georgia
January 1996

CHAPTER 1

———

YOUR
CELL WILL
TEACH YOU

In Scetis, a brother went to see Abba Moses and begged him for a word. And the old man said: Go and sit in your cell, and your cell will teach you everything.[1]

In this brief saying a brother approaches one of the great figures of the desert, Abba Moses. Moses' early life had been an unhappy one. He was a slave from Ethiopia, and presumably a black man. For whatever reason he escaped his early fate only to turn to thievery, laying upon vulnerable travelers and caravans, robbing them, perhaps even murdering at times. Certainly in the desolate regions of Egypt robbery could be tantamount to murder. Abandoning individuals to the arid landscape without provisions

1

or transportation left them precious little hope of reaching the safety of an encampment or village.

Late in life Moses underwent a conversion of heart, became a monk, and submitted to the rigors of training as an ascetic under the venerable Abba Isidore, the priest. Abba Macarius urged him to seek out the solitude of Petra, where Abba Anthony had lived his eremitical life and where Moses was to meet a martyr's death along with seven of his brother hermits.

In this concise saying the brother who seeks out Abba Moses must have heard his impressive story from other monks and hermits. Seeking advice from the revered Abba Moses was more than an inconvenience. It was an arduous undertaking. It required physical as well as spiritual stamina to travel on foot into the desolate region of Petra. But the brother had an urgent request of Abba Moses, whose life resonated in the heart of the suppliant brother pilgrim. He begged the old wise hermit for his advice. He *needed* the elder monk's advice. He wasn't looking for answers to specific problems that regularly crop up in day-to-day living. He was seeking the kind of wisdom that is born of facing the suffering and pathos entangled in the very fact of living on this earth.

The advice he received from Abba Moses could almost be taken as a dismissal of the brother's anxious, even desperate, petition. The brother begged for a word from Abba Moses. After weeks of journeying in the companionship of hunger and thirst, fearful of the wild animals equally hungry and robbers thirsty for bounty, he is told in effect to go back home and stay there: to sit in his cell and learn the lessons that only solitude teaches.

The spare story gives no hint that the brother took offense or was disappointed in Abba Moses' advice. To the contrary, the fact that the story has come down to us indicates that the brother cherished the advice and passed it on to his brother monks and novices. True, Abba Moses didn't address his deepest yearnings or alleviate his suffering, or allay his fears, or read the scroll of his heart and fit its shape with tailored wisdom. Abba Moses gave the brother something more valuable and more easily overlooked in a person's rush for pat answers. He didn't feed the younger monk with eternal wisdom, but rather taught him how to satisfy the hunger that drives us humans into foolishness and trivialities.

And the brother was ready to hear him. The two qualities that are necessary preconditions for this sort of readiness are courage and experience. It isn't at all difficult to imagine that this brother experienced "the wall" in his life. He wasn't like Abba Moses, who might have found the desert of Scetis by accident while hiding during his days as a robber. This brother ran into "the wall," the emptiness that drains off the meaning and joy of living. When the veneer of our humanly conditioned optimism wears thin, we face a harsh reality expressed in the haunting, lingering sense that something terribly important is slipping through our grasp as we age.

Isn't it true of human beings that no matter what we may do, the best of what we name "me" seems to elude our understanding? Why is it that no matter what I do, and even at times do well, I am never satisfied? Why, when I am honest with myself, do I discover that I am always on a hunt, not even particularly knowing what I am hunting for?

This experience of inner restlessness embedded in the minute and multitudinous acts that constitute living is the experience of this dear brother, who sought out the company and advice of Abba Moses, who as a robber was also hunting for an answer to his own restlessness.

Jacob Needleman in *Consciousness and Tradition* tells the story of a New York psychiatrist who experimented with hypnosis on a young soldier who was his patient. He had given the soldier a posthypnotic suggestion that caused him to stomp his foot three times when the psychiatrist snapped his finger. When asked why he had done such an odd thing, the soldier offered a completely rational and wrong explanation: because he had something in his shoe. The psychiatrist goes on to explain the significance of the experiment:

> Do you think the whole of our psychic life is like that?...Do you think that every movement we make, every word we say, every thought we have is like that? Could it be that we are always "fabricating" in a sort of low-grade posthypnotic haze? Because there's one thing I am sure of, though only now do I see its importance: the moment I asked that soldier why he had stamped his foot, there was a split second when he realized that *he* had not *done* anything at all. A moment when he realized that the fact was simply that his foot stamped the ground "all by itself." By asking him why he had stamped his foot, I was in effect suggesting to his mind that *he* had *done* something. In short, I was hypnotizing him—or, rather, I was playing into the general proc-

ess of hypnosis that is going on all the time with all of us from the cradle to the grave. The contradiction made him blush, and the true facts about the foot-stamping were blotted out of awareness.[2]

The soldier could be accused of lying if it weren't for the fact of his hypnosis. In a way he was lying, but it's an unrecognized lie, for it is a shared social lie and thus extremely difficult to detect. Perhaps it isn't so much a lie as it is a web woven around all individuals, entrapping them in a common fiction.

When they began to wake from this shared trance, when they suspected that they were more slaves than free, the men and women of the desert sayings fled their culture to escape the disguises and distractions it perpetrated on their human spirits. It is no small act of courage to face squarely the fictions in our life and the troubling sense that something isn't quite right about our life.

Scapegoating, excuses, self-pity, are common disguises that shield us from a deep-seated doubt. These fictions, these acceptable deceptions, are the way we distract ourselves from the nagging suspicion that at the bottom of what I call "me" is something terribly disturbing. We dare not look into the nooks and crannies of our cupboard because we are afraid that we'll find it's empty.

Human uniqueness is a blessing and a burden, a source of joy and a source of distress, for when all is said and done, we live our lives all alone. When I was very young, I asked my father: How do I know that the color I call "red" is the same color that everyone else calls "red"? How do I know that what I see as red, you don't see as green and someone else sees as blue? This young child wasn't asking the perennial question of epistemology. He was asking something far more fundamental. Am I all alone living in a kind of fool's paradise? What's real? What can I trust? What's permanent? What's reliable? How can I know that we are not all fooling ourselves? Is what is called life nothing more than a common conspiracy to distract us from some terrible reality? How do we confront the suspicion we hardly dare acknowledge that what we consider real, meaningful, authentic, is just a kind of dream, a fiction arising out of a common trance?

This is the urgent issue that the brother wanted Abba Moses to address. Simple answers, pious platitudes, even sincere assurances, won't slake the thirst for genuine advice in the face of this human dilemma. Go sit in your cell, and your cell will teach you everything. Only this kind of humility in the face of transitory existence could meet the brother's disconcerting experience of life. Abba Moses' wisdom is a sounding of the depth of the human experience. As we follow it down into the inner reaches of human awareness, we discover that his advice blossoms into layers of meaning.

"Sit in your cell" means on the surface to shut yourself in a space defined by four walls and a ceiling. It is a voluntary imprisonment not as penance or retribution, but as recognition that we are scattered over a range of minor and distracting concerns. Retreating from the active life—or, more accurately, an overly active one—into a cell physically cuts off disorienting and hypnotizing "worldly" concerns. It is a concrete acknowledgment that the self is ill at ease.

Abba Moses' advice also points to something deeper and inner. "Cell" means "self" as well. Sit in yourself! Just as you'd learn every detail of a hermitage if you never left it over three or four years, so you'll learn every detail of yourself. In this living cell we learn the discord between how I think of myself, how I sense myself to be, and how I behave. We learn that consciousness is not synonymous with its content, that thoughts and impulses and emotions come and go, but consciousness itself is like the stage on which these actors play out their parts. We discover something of our self that we cannot quite grasp, a subtle sense of "I am" that endures no matter what else of us changes. This brings us to the doorway of a vast and liberating emptiness that is more positive than any verbal, mental, or emotional assertion of self can ever hope to be. This threshold leads to what is so overwhelmingly positive that images and descriptions of it pale like stars upon the arrival of morning light.

There is a final sense to the word "cell," meaning "the liberated self," wherein life becomes transparent and obvious. The differences in forms remain, of course, but since the self is transparent, there are no barriers between forms. This very existence in all its multiplicity of expression at this very moment is "it" altogether all at once. It is what the human heart craves, and it has always been obvious. "Your cell" has no walls, neither physical ones of mortar or wood, nor walls of flesh and bone, nor psychological ones defining a separate, independent self. The marketplace is your cell.

Abba Moses' "cell" is a metaphor for the imprisoned self. If our appetite for the truth is strong enough to shore

up our crumbling courage battered by the relentless onslaught of life's experiences, then we are rewarded by the
emergence of the essence behind what is considered our
self.

To break down the wisdom in Abba Moses' response so
we can mentally digest it is to miss the point. For it isn't
that "it" must, or even can, become understandable to us.
It is we who must become transparent to "it," much as
Saint John of the Cross indicated in his simile of the sun
passing unimpeded through a clean, clear windowpane.

If we accustomedly flee our loneliness and the lessons it
has to teach us, hiding behind the excitement around us
and in social company, then we will likely greet Abba Moses'
advice with a goodly portion of dread. If, on the other hand,
we are weary of the shallow trivialities of the social order
and afflicted by the inane discourse of most human com-
munication, then we are likely to feel relief at the advice
"Go and sit in your cell." Whichever way we react, we do
not enter our cell alone.

CHAPTER 2

WHO AM I?

Abba Poemen said to Abba Joseph: Tell me how I can become a monk. And he replied: If you want to find rest here and hereafter, say in every occasion, who am I? and do not judge anyone.[1]

Abba Poemen is one of the most gifted of the early desert hermits. He was noted for his moderation and refreshing common sense during a time when penitential extremes were considered admirable. He tempered enthusiasm for the ascetical life by encouraging hermits to take sufficient nourishment daily instead of fasting for days on end. Love of others took precedence over everything, including the rigorous observance of the hermit's silence. Once when he was consulted regarding the disturbances of the devil, Abba Poemen replied: "Devil! It is always the devil that's to blame. I say it is self-will."[2] It was this utterly practical man who approached the venerable Abba Joseph for advice.

The novice Poemen, newly arrived in the desert, had enough awareness and courage to realize that he was a fractured and scattered individual. The translation of his question to Abba Joseph doesn't do justice to the texture of his request. The root of the Greek word for "monk," *monos,* means "one" or "singular," and carries the sense of "completeness" or "wholeness." He was in effect asking Abba Joseph: How can I be whole?

One of the first fruits of a solitary life is the sharp awareness that what I assumed to be "me" is not singular. Being alone is like living in a large family that is never quite at peace with itself. It is just like some of the dreams we have, peopled with all kinds of characters, more than we can count, and each with their own personalities, playing out their dream roles. One is wise, another foolish; one is compassionate, another vicious and dangerous; one compliant and happy and carefree, while others are vulnerable, wounded, or depressed. Our inner family, what we call ourselves, is made up of opposites that aren't quite at ease together.

Young Poemen found himself taking sides, preferring some of the "family members" over others, and others still he hardly acknowledged at all. His view and ideal of himself was skewed in favor of what comforted him. What he discovered, however, was that promoting his likable characteristics was a flawed strategy. Trying to shape his undesirable traits to his preferences was like trying to grasp beaded pools of mercury on a slick table surface. How do you make this group that is too often at odds with itself whole?

Each human being is endowed with a guardian who protects the boundaries of the self. Psychology calls this human function the ego. It isn't a "thing" or a small entity residing in some mysterious recesses of the psyche. It's a talent for organizing experiences and staking out the self's inner and outer territory, for identifying personal needs and preferences, and for recognizing what's mine and what's not. It is our capacity to believe that we are different from everyone and everything else, a belief that isn't untrue but isn't entirely accurate either.

There are many necessary benefits accruing from the guardian ego. It permits us to deliberate on our experiences, to set goals, to grasp the unwritten rules of our cultural heritage, allowing us to be effective in a particular social matrix, to control our impulses and master ourselves, to organize our thoughts, to embrace and embody values that are personally and socially beneficial, and most important, it gives us a sense of congruence with our biographical experiences.

Meditation is a natural ally of the guardian ego, reinforcing the sense of an independent and separate self. There is nothing particularly mysterious about meditation. Human beings, perhaps without being fully conscious of it, meditate on themselves continually. It is a kind of psychological grooming, or self-monitoring, to ensure that the guardian ego's catalog of the self's traits remain intact and its boundaries sound. In short, human beings become the subjects of their meditation: themselves, or at least themselves as they've come to understand themselves. For better or worse, we reap what we sow in self-meditation.

If there are benefits, there are also limits in the functional talent called the ego. To define ourselves is not only to say who or what we are but also what we are not, an attempt to make ourselves invulnerable and permanent. Once the self is defined and organized, all kinds of problems leap into existence. Everything we exclude from our self-definition becomes a potential threat. We are then on watch with the aid of sober judgment, reason's contribution to maintaining the mirage of the separate self we've staked out, discreetly comparing and evaluating everything and everyone as friend or foe. Fear and yearning compose the atmosphere that our sentinel self breathes. Fear is the footprint of our attempt to make ourselves invulnerable and yearning the footprint of our attempt to make ourselves permanent.

The guardian ego is a scriptwriter, tagging moods, experiences, behaviors, and things as "me," keeping a record of its biographical inventory, which it stores in memory. Since it is a mental function, however, all it can really come up with is an *idea* of the self, which it eventually fashions into an *ideal*—and unfortunately too often into an *idol*. Its attempt to feed and keep the idol intact is narcissism in its purest form—the worship of the self-idol.

The self-idol is little more than a deep trance circumscribing awareness, keeping us in a fog about our real identity. It mirrors back and reinforces what we already know about ourselves, keeping at bay what is us but doesn't fit the idol's image. The self-idol is essentially a highly edited version of who I am, and the guardian ego is essentially a place marker. It's entirely up to us where we put our thumb in the pages of our life experiences.

Despite all the talent and effort of the guardian ego, we are not one. We are many in ourselves. We live in a cast of characters residing in the wings of consciousness. We bring these characters out to center stage when we feel the need for them. And we throw ourselves into the roles with vigor and conviction. What good actors we are, living through these pseudo selves, or is it that we are lived by them? Who, we may legitimately ask, is in charge here? Who is coordinating the cast, who is choreographing the play, who is asking the question, and who is reading this text?

Me! we are quick to answer. But who is that? My awareness? What happens to "me" when I fall asleep or lose consciousness? Am I my personality? My talents? My preferences? My physical shape and weight? My history? A simple accident that damages the frontal lobe of the brain, or the onslaught of Alzheimer's disease, can erase all the traits and patterns that I consider to be me, like the accidental deletion of data from a computer disk. So who am I when you take away all the props and rehearsed answers? One thing for certain, I am not an easy object of inquiry—or an object of any kind, for that matter. I am a subject (but what is a subject?) that I temporarily objectify in order to investigate it.

In defining ourselves well, we have let something fall between the cracks. I am more than a collection of historical facts and incidents, a list of vital statistics and passionate attachments, more than a coagulation of preferences and aversions and rutted patterns of reactions, more than that elusive sense of something subsisting behind the scenes so to speak of everything I can observe and assert about myself. Mystics who relentlessly pursued the question want us to go even deeper than these slippery identities.

Beyond the capacity of the guardian ego, we may have a disconcerting sense, when we are alone, that someone or something else has fallen in between our crafted self-definition. We are especially aware of this when a dream scrambles the events of our life in a disturbing manner and we intuitively know that it is showing us something of ourselves we've missed, but we can't quite make sense of it. Intellectual curiosity yields only a bunch of fragments in our quest for self-understanding. And if we glued them all together in humpty-dumpty fashion, the aggregate would yet leave us wondering: Who am I? Wondering what has fallen in between the fragments summoned the young, restless Poemen to the feet of Abba Joseph to learn what had eluded his self-mastery and understanding.

This kind of ignorance and the anguish it inflicts on us is not a desirable condition. But the acknowledgment of our ignorance and anguish is indeed desirable, for it is the necessary precondition to learning. Its message is that the space we staked out for ourselves is too narrow, too small, too tiny. Just as a child in a womb or a teenager at home must leave the comfort and safety of the known, so we must leave the security of our well-defined self, for its environment is temporary. It is fitted to a task, and when that is accomplished, it's time to move on. How do we know when it is time? The environment turns inimical with disturbing dissatisfactions and vague yearnings for some unknown "more."

Our anguish is double-edged. It is the pain of being cramped into too narrow a space, like wearing shoes that are too tight. It is also the fruit of our denial of the transcendent. We burden our defined self with the weight of the transcendent, trying to make this square peg fit a round hole. How we've shaped ourselves is both inadequate and inaccurate. A great obstacle to seeing this is that the guardian ego, which brooks no competition, has given us such great benefits. At its best it made us independent, self-reliant, and responsible. It gives us an appropriate sense of power and worth, along with a degree of comfort and familiarity leading to expertise, skill, and the pleasure of living well, but not necessarily living well-off.

Our well-defined self can't address our need for the transcendent. It neglects the infinite and eternal since both exceed the grasp of the guardian ego. As long as we are engaged in interesting and practical tasks, purpose and meaning attend to this separate-self sense, but in an arbitrary and fleeting fashion. What happens to life in between the accomplishments? What happens to life when we can't be useful, when there is nothing to do, when we're faced with the tragic and the poignant? What happens to life when our skills are useless, leaving us helpless? The guardian ego can no more carry the weight of the transcendent than a fetus can bear the burdens and joys of an adult. It is by nature exclusive, and what it has excluded is the self too, unrecognized and unacknowledged. The life it engenders is but a shadow of the life envisioned in the gospels: "I have come that you might have life and have it to the full."

We have censored our vision rather than look carefully

enough at the reality that is ourselves. We are required to inspect ourselves far more carefully and closely than we have yet dared. And what is even more disconcerting, we must both do it alone and in a way we have so far avoided. We must forsake the comfortable and no longer deny what is becoming obvious— the anguish of living is inherent in the guardian ego and our self-definition. The background of our self-definition, the foil behind the stage on which we play out our life, the canvas under the vivid colors that shape our self-image, summons our attention, requiring us to leave behind the familiar sense of self the guardian ego has built up.

When the novice Poemen looked carefully at himself, he saw that he was simply an adolescent in the spiritual life, sometimes tossed about by the stormy confusion of his passions or, what is worse, resigned to a life of rutted boredom occasionally pockmarked by religious enthusiasm. He was perplexed and disturbed at the sight of his neglect, but he had run out of scapegoats and excuses. He could no longer divert his gaze from the companion suffering of the guardian ego or distract himself from the point his discontent brought home to him by setting out on the task of acquiring more. In the end such a strategy is a dead-end street, since "more" will turn on him and eat away what little contentment he has achieved. More comfort makes us softer; more pleasure, jaded; more wealth, stingy; more security, fearful and fretful; more self-esteem, narcissistic.

Abba Joseph addressed a young man trapped by his own restlessness. His great compassion and wisdom wouldn't allow him to siphon off the discontent. Rather, he saw it as the causeway to a deeper peace than human efforts can achieve. He instructed the young Poemen on how to learn: "If you want to find rest here and hereafter, say in every occasion: who am I? and do not judge anyone."

As is so often the case with the desert sayings, it is deceptively simple advice carrying a double dose of wisdom. Abba Joseph's advice to the young Poemen is to continue on the course he has followed. He uses Poemen's natural talent for self-inquiry, employing it for a higher goal, beyond the reach of the guardian ego. Poemen's fidelity to the practice will cut a swath to the transcendent.

First of all, the advice "do not judge anyone" cuts to the very heart of the guardian ego, which exists for the purpose of discriminating. There is a very fine line between labeling and condemning that is too easily and unconsciously crossed. Labeling someone as different easily translates into good or bad, right or wrong, and any variation between these opposites. Judging erects barriers—subtle ones perhaps, but obstacles nonetheless. Not judging means sidestepping the function of the guardian ego by avoiding its tainted labels placed over myself, others, and life's circumstances.

Not judging is no easy task. We are not only taught at an early age to discriminate in everything, we are subconsciously accustomed to it and reinforce our habit of it almost on a moment-by-moment basis. Perhaps because it is so difficult, it is an injunction in the gospels: Do not judge and you will not be judged.

The task the young Poemen received from Abba Joseph was to abandon the judgments he was leveling against him-

self. What was he to do? Nothing. Just to notice those quirks
that had irked him and made him restless, and to notice his
reaction to them. But let them be, and let himself be. After
a while he will give up his resistance to his undesirable traits
and settle down with himself. Then he will be able to learn
to love all of himself, not just those aspects the guardian
ego cherishes so much. Behind the guardian ego and its
discriminations is the bare self, which is naturally at ease
and nonjudgmental.

The second part of Abba Joseph's advice, "Say in every
occasion, who am I?" is a spiritual practice that has the
power of a drop of acid on the iron surface of the guardian
ego. It requires stillness, internal silence, monotonous repetition, and commitment. The practice is designed to eliminate distractions from the work by training the attention to
the point of a unified consciousness.

The answer to the question "who am I?" is usually an
exercise in memory. We keep reminding ourselves of who
we are, keep reinforcing our identities. The question is,
however, who am I now before I can think about it? In-
quire into the question "Who am I?" without judging or
determining the answer. One must reject all answers until
one has reached the obvious, for anything that I see is an
object of inquiry and thus not the subject inquiring.

Carefully look for the answer beyond the parameters
you have called yourself. It is always present and obvious,
but comes at the price of the guardian ego. The natural
curiosity about the mystery of ourselves can be cultivated
into a spiritual skill and talent for the transcendent. It is
called "transcendent" because it goes beyond the conven-

tional capacity of the human intellect, beyond the guarding and organizing capacity of the personality.

Abba Joseph's advice is much like "The Wood Cutter's Story":

> At the edge of a forest lived a man who made a humble living chopping kindling and selling it to his neighbors. One day a hermit came out of the forest, and the man asked him for some advice. "Go deeper into the woods," the hermit replied. And so the man did—and found wonderful, large trees, which he felled and sold as lumber. Having become wealthy, one day he remembered the advice of the hermit, "Go deeper into the woods." And so he went farther on and came to a silver mine that he worked and became wealthier still. Then again, one day he remembered the hermit's advice and so went on even farther into the woods. There he came upon a precious stone on the forest floor. He admired its brilliance and remembered the advice of the hermit, "Go deeper into the forest." One day he found himself at the edge of the forest where he had long ago met the hermit. Happy as never before, he picked up his ax and began cutting kindling once again.

The answer to the question isn't at the bottom of one's search. It is not buried under layers of fiction. It is not behind historical data or vital statistics or woven into the self-idol or in the enigma of one's dreams. Bypass the guardian ego, and instantly the answer is obvious. It is nothing in particular, not this, not that. It is like ice and water or the wave and the ocean. It is not so much a matter of the relationship between them, but of the connaturality of the two.

There are numerous stories from the desert where the monk, after enduring great asceticism—fasts, penances, vigils—turns up healthy and whole. Our skewed view of ourselves and our needs has obscured what is both necessary and beneficial to physical existence. Man does not live by bread alone. The spirit shines through, radiates from the body, not that the bone structures change or muscle tone increases, but that something far more subtle, something that is both ageless and incorruptible, radiates through human existence.

CHAPTER 3

—

IN THE
BEGINNING...

*Amma Syncletica said: In the beginning, there is
struggle and a lot of work for those who come
near to God. But after that, there is indescribable joy. It is just like building a fire: at first it's
smoky and your eyes water, but later you get the
desired result. Thus we ought to light the divine
fire in ourselves with tears and effort.*[1]

Our sense of a separate enduring self is a con-
vention—a designation chosen at some level
of our being—that is momentarily useful. The arbitrary
nature of the separate self sense doesn't mean that there is
no self here. It means that there is no *knowable* self here,
for what we call our self is as mysterious and as elusive
as what we call God. We give it all kinds of names and
definitions and descriptions, but the finest minds and

wisest hearts in religion have warned us that our designa-
tions conceal far more than they reveal about either ourselves or God.

Western culture has particularly developed well and encourages reliance on our intellectual capacities. But this is
the very thing that also encourages the sense we have of a
separate enduring self, a sense that acts like a deeply embedded trance, both obscuring and distorting the truth about
ourselves. If thinking is our only tool, then everything looks
like an idea, the very thing the functional talent called the
ego serves up to us. But we already saw that even accurate
ideas of ourselves, while beneficial, are inadequate.

Thinking and the deep self-trance are as inseparable as
up and down, left and right, and cold and heat. Without
"left" you'd never know "right," without "up," "down"
would make no sense, and without "heat" you couldn't
feel "cold." Thinking and the deep self-trance are as bound
together as fire and smoke. Where there's fire, there's smoke,
and where there's thinking, there's the deep self-trance.

The question of vital importance is: What can I do to
dispel the trance? The problem is that the very act of thinking, regardless of whether it is right or wrong, creates the
deep self-trance in the first place. Our capacity to think
well is like a host for the deep self-trance parasite. So whatever I do cannot involve thinking, which just reinforces the
very trance I'm trying to overcome.

> Theophilus of holy memory, the bishop of Alexan-
> dria, journeyed to Scetis, and the brethren coming
> together said to Abba Pambo: Say a word or two to

the bishop that his soul may be edified in this place.
The elder replied: If he is not edified by my silence,
there is no hope that he will be edified by my words.[2]

It will be helpful to carefully adhere to Abba Joseph's
advice: Do not judge anyone. Describing the deep self-trance
metaphorically as a parasite gives the impression that it must
be something bad. Neither the host nor the parasite is bad.
They are bound, and strengthening the host is strengthening the parasite, albeit unintentionally. Feeding the one transfers nourishment and energy to the other. We deal with it
not because it is bad, but because it is incomplete and limits
our freedom to live life to the full.

How do we break out of this? We must do something
that our culture says, wrongly, is impossible, or at least in-
advisable. We must take up a practice that can only be described as "nonthinking." Nonthinking sounds like a dead-
end street, but it isn't. Everything in us says that it's wrong,
causing us to greet this advice with perplexed disbelief.
Nonthinking isn't a matter of giving up thinking or having
a blank mind. It's a matter of overcoming the *habitual conflict* that composes thinking. Amma Syncletica was referring to this when she said:

> There are many who live in the mountains and be-
> have as if they were in the town, and they are wast-
> ing their time. It is possible to be a solitary in one's
> mind while living in a crowd, and it is possible for
> one who is a solitary to live in the crowd of his
> own thoughts.[3]

The sense of a separate self is so embedded in the habitual conflict composing thinking that thinking and our independence seem to be the same thing. Even children recognize this when they are frightened of a dark bedroom. They fear that they will lose control over their habit of thinking and that goblins await them in the dark to gulp them up from their own beds. Sophisticated adults follow the same childhood pattern when they fear being gobbled up by someone else's ideas, career, or emotional life, a fear that sets the rule of thumb that if we can't think for ourselves, we aren't independent. For this reason Amma Syncletica says that the first steps toward genuine freedom are very difficult ones indeed, for we fear jeopardizing something essential to our sense of self.

There are practices specifically designed to thwart the habit of thinking, making this difficult task easier. They have been tried and perfected over centuries and across cultures, and validated again and again by vastly different personalities whom history has recognized as genuinely free and wholesome individuals. They are meant to set us up for a fall. They act like a net cast over the guardian ego, trapping it in the grip of the transcendent, where our sense of a separate self falls away before the Absolute.

The author of *The Cloud of Unknowing* explains one element of a practice this way:

> ...take just a little word, of one syllable rather than of two; for the shorter it is the better it is in agreement with this exercise of the spirit. Such a one is the word "God" or the word "love." Choose which

one you prefer, or any other according to your liking—the word of one syllable that you like best. Fasten this word to your heart, so that whatever happens it will never go away. This word is to be your shield and your spear, whether you are riding in peace or in war. With this word you are to beat upon this cloud and this darkness above you. With this word you are to strike down every kind of thought under the cloud of forgetting....[4]

In *The Interior Castle* Saint Teresa of Avila tells us about the prayer of Brother Masseo, an early follower of Saint Francis of Assisi:

Often when he was praying, he would express his joy in a soft constant cooing sound like a gentle dove: "Ooo-Ooo." And he would remain in contemplation that way, with a joyful expression on his face and a happy heart.[5]

The important point of these quotations is not so much *which* word is used, but the simplicity of the practice itself. *The Cloud of Unknowing* states clearly that it doesn't matter which monosyllabic word you choose for a practice. What is vital is "to strike down every kind of thought under the cloud of forgetting," which means that the habit of thinking is bypassed in the monotonous repetition of the chosen word. Brother Masseo seems to have stumbled upon a technique that is very helpful, at least in the beginning. The sound he uses, "Ooo-Ooo," carries no intellectual content and thus is less likely to evoke mental images or a line of thought, both of which could distract him from the practice itself. This is the meaning of the desert saying "An old man said, 'Constant prayer quickly straightens out our thoughts.'"[6]

Another traditional element of a practice, which concerns the way a practitioner breathes, has a direct bearing on the habit of thinking. It will probably surprise most people when they hear that the mind doesn't control thoughts very well, if at all. But the breath controls thoughts and the thinking process quite effectively. You can validate the truth of this by your own experience. If you inhale moderately and hold your breath for a few seconds, you will notice that your thought process stopped momentarily. The more naturally disciplined breathing is, the more congruent the practice will be.

Breathing correctly forms the anchor for a proficient practice. One doesn't have to learn any special or complicated techniques for breathing correctly. One has to unlearn all the bad breathing habits acquired since early childhood. Most adults physically express their anxiety in breathing, using only the upper-chest area instead of allowing the solar plexus to expand and contract naturally with each inhalation and exhalation. Notice how a child breathes naturally with the stomach fully extended and imitate that which you have forgotten in the hustle and bustle of adult responsibilities.

Counting the breath is an effective method for combining correct breathing and the practice recommended by *The Cloud of Unknowing*. The value of breath counting lies in the fact that reasoning and mental activity recede into the background in the attentiveness to the breath counting. Beyond the mechanics of breath counting, the heart of the matter is to be completely absorbed by the practice like a child absorbed in play. When counting "one," let there be only "one" in the whole universe, and so forth with "two," etc. In this way the waves of thought are stilled, the spirit is put at rest, and over time a clear and sharp "one-pointedness" is gradually established in the mind, a condition that runs counter to the usual habit of thinking.

In a formal contemplative setting it will be helpful to allot twenty-five minutes to the practice of breath counting. At the beginning of the twenty-five minutes take a couple of deep and natural breaths. Fill the lungs to their capacity, letting them push out the stomach all the way, and then let your breath "fall" out, slowly and easily. Then begin to count the exhalations, letting the inhalations pass without counting them. When you exhale, count inwardly "won-n-n," inhale, and on the next exhalation count "two-oo-oo," inhale, and on the next exhalation count "three-ee-ee," and so forth up to ten. Repeat the count from one to ten on each exhalation for the length of the twenty-five minutes, starting over at "one" after each tenth breath. In the beginning or at times of inner agitation, it can be helpful to use this method in counting both the inhalations and exhalations. (After the practice of breath counting is well established, you may find it helpful to count only the inhalations, allowing the exhalations to pass without counting them.)

In the middle of the counting, some other idea may likely erupt in your head, and you will find yourself involved with it for a while. However, you will soon return to yourself and take up the counting again; but now you discover that you have forgotten where you left off and must go back to the beginning and start from "one" again. Everyone who has tried this practice for the first time must have experienced this failure and been surprised by the inability to control thoughts as he or she wanted.

At first you will be very conscious of each step in this procedure, but eventually breath counting will become second nature to you. It takes time, perhaps months or longer, for this practice to establish itself, and you may seem at first to spend most of your time daydreaming rather than counting. It is quite normal for the brain to be active as it is for the lung to be active in a person who is alive. So don't condemn yourself for this normal condition.

Thoughts that naturally flit across the mind are not in themselves an impediment to a practice such as this. There is a general misconception that this practice aims to get rid of all thoughts. This is quite a flawed understanding. No matter how intently you count your breath, you will still see what is in your line of vision when your eyes are opened, and you will hear the normal sounds about you. And since you are not asleep, various thought patterns will dart about in your mind.

These do not hamper or diminish the effectiveness of practice unless, evaluating them as good, you cling to them, or deciding that they are bad, you try to eliminate them. Just let random thoughts arise and vanish as they will. Do not dally with them and do not try to expel them. Merely concentrate on counting your breath with all your attention.

Traditionally the contemplative practitioner sat on a stool or low bench.[7] More recently Westerners have learned the benefit of either the full crossed-legged sitting posture or one of the modifications of it. Much patient practice and experimentation may be necessary to learn how to sit well this way, but the advantages are well worth one's efforts and troubles. It will clarify your mind, dispel the fuzzy web of confusion, and keep your thoughts from wandering about.

A number of different sitting postures can be used during a formal practice, and the student should experiment to discover which suits him or her best. The easier ones can be used in the earlier stages of practice. It doesn't matter what posture is adopted, provided the student can maintain a straight spine and a stable, motionless position without serious discomfort for twenty to thirty minutes. In the beginning, if there is any doubt or hesitation about posture, it is probably best for Westerners to sit in a chair, keeping the spine straight.

The upper part of the body floats on a pivot somewhere in the area of the base of the spine. When you sit for a formal practice, bend forward, thrust out your buttocks, and let the upper part of your body rest on that pivot. Then you can relax the upper part of the body into the position. The chin should be tucked in as far as possible, to the point where you feel that you are beginning to choke off your breath a bit. With the crown of your head, try to touch the ceiling. This will straighten your spine. At this point the whole upper part of your body should be floating on the pivot at the base of the spine. Then "sink" into the cushion or chair.

A final element is a personal commitment, which is like a lubricant on the mechanism of a practice. Commitment is the courage to stick to the practice all the way to the end, all the way to the loss of the guardian ego's power over us. It is not unusual to begin a practice like this with flawed motives: to be considered someone special, to get the attention of someone important, to feel good about oneself, or simply to get relief from the tensions of modern living. Whatever your motives, they will become clear as you continue and deepen your practice.

At that time a disillusionment with yourself will set in, and you will feel like giving up the whole endeavor. That would be a grave mistake, because what is happening is that the practice is purifying you, and it is both a significant step along the way and an encouraging sign. There will be many times in the practice when you will be tempted to give it up. And there will always be a handy excuse to lure you away from the practice. Without commitment you would not return to your practice again and again. The best advice comes from the desert sayings: "Abba Poemen said about Abba Pior that every single day he made a fresh beginning."[8] There are in the end only three stages to this work: to be a beginner, to be more of a beginner, and to be only a beginner.

Applying the analogy of travel here, the point is to put down your money, buy your ticket, pack your bags, and make the journey. Watching a travelogue won't do. It is only then, when we are resolved to see the work through to the end despite all the difficulties, that we get the desired results. Without practice all instructions are worthless, like sheet music that is never played, a choreographic score that is never danced, or a fire that is never lit.

A brother came to Abba Theodore and spent three days begging him to say a word to him without getting any reply. So he went away grieved. The old man's disciple said to him, "Abba, why did you not say a word to him? See, he has gone away grieved." The old man said to him, "I did not speak to him, for he is a trafficker who seeks to glorify himself through the words of others."[9]

A practice such as the one described here can accelerate what happens over a lifetime if we do it attentively. The longer you live, the more you learn that you cannot control your life very much. You are in control of very little, as a matter of fact. The more you realize this fact, the more likely you will enjoy life, the natural ecstasy inherent in life itself. This doesn't mean that the external circumstances bend to your pleasure. It means you cease judging life, and circumstances, and events, on the basis of your personal comfort and desires. The religious traditions call this "living the Will of God." Then something happens, something indescribable. We are living in the Mystery, or perhaps to say it better, the Mystery is living us.

CHAPTER 4

NONATTACHMENT

When Abba Macarius was in Egypt, he found a man with a mule stealing his belongings. Then, as though he were a stranger, he helped the robber to load the animal, and peacefully sent him off, saying: "We have brought nothing into the world, and we cannot take anything with us. The Lord has given, and as he has wished, so it has happened. Blessed be the Lord in all things."[1]

The last chapter described the components of a practice that can help us get beyond the artificial limits we place around ourselves. Posture, breathing, attitude, and breath counting are like ingredients for a recipe that require proper mixing and oven baking until done. There is nothing particularly mystifying about this kind of practice. It is eminently explicable. Catholic spiritual tradition calls it "acquired contemplation"; this is nothing other than developing a skill, which can get frustrating and boring. That's just the way life is.

Learning any skill, of course, entails a certain amount of trouble, which is why all learning involves ritual. When you pay someone to teach you anything, you will be taught a set of rituals commensurate with the skills you want to learn. In the secular sphere these rituals are called techniques, but it doesn't matter whether they are called techniques or rituals, for the end results are the same. The repetition of the components of the desired skill over the course of time allows the practitioner to balance all of the elements in an unselfconscious way.

If you want to improve your golf game, you go to the local pro and pay him an hourly fee. Probably the first thing he asks you to do is to swing the club a few times while he watches your performance. If your stance is stiff and tense, he is liable to tell you to learn to relax, and your first lesson may not involve anything that bears directly on hitting golf balls, much less hitting them well. Then, as you progress, he will teach you various techniques for addressing the ball, swinging the club, and other "advanced" tricks to counter the "natural" tendencies you have that are defeating your golf game. The interesting thing is that even golfers who are winning hundreds of thousands of dollars a year on pro tours regularly go to someone to teach them how to swing a club.

Skill alone doesn't make championship golfers, nor does it awaken meditative practitioners to Ultimate Reality. Rituals, or techniques, aim at something beyond the skill itself—that is, beyond the control of the individual. If a person cannot make anything happen, why practice these rather annoying techniques? Think of it this way; if awakening to Ultimate Reality is like an accident, then this acquired contemplation is like standing in the middle of the road. Now standing in the middle of the road does not guarantee that you will be hit by a car, any more than standing on the side of the road guarantees that you won't be hit by a car. However, if you do stand in the middle of the road, you are more likely, though not assuredly, to get hit by a car than if you stand on the side of the road. If you faithfully continue your practice, you are putting yourself in line with the grace of Union with God.

An essential element in developing the skills of acquired contemplation is one's personal effort to be completely absorbed in the practice. The rituals are only adjuncts to that. Furthermore, acquired contemplation at best, which produces a certain kind of natural tranquillity in the practitioner, disposes one for the grace of Union with God. The grace of Union with God is just that, *gratis*, unearned, undeserved, and given whenever the benefactor chooses to give the gift, to whomever he chooses to give it.

Just as playing golf well is not a matter of intention per se, so too contemplation is not a matter of intention—although intention does perform a small role in both. Rather, contemplation is entirely a matter of *attention*—that is, doing the practice in as unselfconscious a manner as possible, because the quality of the attention counts for much. If one is simply satisfied with the natural tranquillity yielded up by acquired contemplation, then one is satisfied with a half-baked practice that may quickly go rancid. The essence of a mature practice is to lose the self in the practice. Beyond the mechanics and techniques the heart of the practice is to let there be only "one" in the whole universe when we count one, and only "two" in the whole universe when we count two.

Another word for this quality of attention is "non-attachment," which doesn't necessarily refer to extreme ascetical behavior. Nonattachment is the attitude that comes from the acceptance of the fact that everything about my life and in my life comes and goes in its own time regardless of my preferences or aversions. It is an attitude that allows us to cooperate with the natural rhythm of life.

Trying to keep relationships, pleasant experiences, a sense of security, youth, or anything else from their natural rhythms is both disruptive and detrimental to ourselves and to others. Anything that we hold onto will throw us off balance and eventually kill us if we persist in possessing it. Take the breath, for example. You cannot be attached to a breath and live. You must let your breath go, let your lungs empty out, in order to be refreshed by the next breath. The same goes for food. You cannot retain food and live. Your body has to get rid of it. How often do people make themselves physically and emotionally ill in their attempt to preserve or create a certain quality in a relationship or in their attempt to duplicate a special experience that gave them a sense of liberation? Nonattachment not only honors the rhythm inherent in life itself, it also frees us to experience life in this temporal realm on its own terms.

Nonattachment is far more subtle and profound than a refined disdain for or emotional indifference to events and people. It doesn't mean that we change our likes into dislikes and our dislikes into likes. It doesn't even have anything to do with wanting and not wanting. It has everything to do with "I" want and "I" don't want. It is letting go of the "I" in the wanting and not wanting. In the words of Saint Thomas More, it means not taking seriously "this bothersome thing I call myself." Nonattachment does not mean we give up things or people or reputation. It means we give up the self.

It seems that we humans are motivated by two "sets" of emotions. The first kind are upwellings of energy in response to particular immediate circumstances. When we are startled by a sound or by pain in our finger on a hot pot handle, a surge of energy we label "fear" causes us to reflexively shout out and pull back. When we are unexpectedly insulted or put down, a surge of energy we label "anger" rushes to the defense and causes us to push away. We hasten to protect a child who is about to put his or her finger into an electrical socket. When we are innocently saying or doing something that is offensive to another, a spontaneous surge of energy we label "shame" causes us to immediately attempt to rectify our mistake or clarify our intentions.

This set of emotions is quite natural and useful. We are equipped with energy beneficial to our well-being. This energy is in service of the organism's well-being. The emotions surge up, accomplish what they need to, and then quickly fade out.

The second "set" of emotions is in service of the deep self-trance. This second "set" looks identical to the first but is really the expression of ego resistance, the deep self-trance impeding any encroachment on its domain. Here the emotions are anchored in resisting change, resisting lack of control, resisting anything that is not "I."

This second set, unlike the first, which is spontaneous and immediate, lingers around in the shadows. But most important, it has a "double face." One side is the face of the deep self-trance, acting like a guard. The other side is the face of the transcendent, acting like a guide. As a guard, it resists any loss of control, any attempt to disturb the deep self-trance. But as a guide, it is a way through the self-trance into the deeper realms of the transpersonal Ultimate Reality.

"This bothersome thing I call myself" finds protection behind three basic emotions: fear, shame, and anger. Anger kicks in when someone (myself or another) does something, which we think can be rectified, that violates the personal deep self-trance patterns. We feel it is "wrong," and here "wrong" means out of step with what my deep self-trance expects or demands. Most of our anger is due to our perception that others have not lived up to our expectations. Occasionally we are angry at ourselves for the same reason. But it is so much easier and more satisfying to be angry at others.

Shame is an emotion that would have us believe we are deficient in our behavior. It generally shows up in our attacking ourselves for being stupid, ignorant, or selfish. We think we have to be other than what we are: We have to be all-wise, all-knowing, all self-giving. This kind of idealism is just a way of gaining the approval of others. We need others' approval when we do not know ourselves, do not accept ourselves.

Shame indicates that I'm not acting in accord with my deep self-trance comfort patterns. My behavior might indeed be morally good, psychologically healthy, and emotionally beneficial, but if it doesn't fit "the learned patterns" permitted by the deep self-trance, then I'm likely to experience a goodly portion of shame until I change my wicked ways. Shame is what we feel when we've done something wrong, when our behavior has been deficient.

Our fundamental fear tells us that we are deficient and incomplete, and that we must look for something (or someone) outside ourselves to achieve wholeness. Our underlying fear is that we are unlovable as we are. Terror is the soil out of which the deep self-trance grows, keeping us on a short leash, shrinking our identity down to the size of our fear. When we let go of this terror, then we discover what is behind this notion of an independent self, we discover who we really are. The externals of life might be tranquil or tumultuous, but the inner life we enjoy is serene and free.

The alternatives to fear, shame, and anger aren't safety, goodness, and peace. Life is insecure, but we don't have to be trapped in fear of it. Rarely is our idea of ourselves equal to the reality of ourselves, but we don't have to be mired in shame about it. Nobody does things right, even most of the time. Most people do the best they can. Even if we think someone's best is inadequate, we don't need to be driven by anger over it.

The source of our fear, shame, and anger is an insecurity about ourselves. When we see through and let go of fear, shame, and anger, what we enter then is not tranquillity, but our insecurity, letting go of the way we think we should be. This is nonattachment—letting go of the self, the self shrunk to the size of our most painful emotions.

Amma Syncletica knew very well this letting go of our shrunken self when she said:

It is good not to get angry. But if it should happen, do not allow your day to go by affected by it. For it is said: Do not let the sun go down. Otherwise, the rest of your life may be affected by it. Why hate a person who hurts you, for it is not that person who is unjust but the devil. Hate the sickness, but not the sick person.

To take our deep self-trance, this shrunken self, seriously is simply to lie to ourselves. We lie to ourselves out of fear. We are afraid of who we really are, although there is no justification for such fear. It is the same kind of fear—the same fear actually—we felt as a child, fear of the fictitious bogeyman.

The deep self-trance uses the emotions to weave a web of substantiality. One doesn't avoid emotions by trying to avoid emotions. What happens is that a person builds up a resistance to fully experiencing life as it is, and this resistance itself is the deep self-trance in action. In letting go, in nonattachment, the very first letting go has to be letting go the resistance to experiencing life as it is, not as I fear it is or hope it to be.

Strange as it may seem, these same emotions that trap us in our unhappiness are guides to the transcendent. It all depends on how we view them—as resistance to change in our personal status quo or as invitations to surrender our ego control. In light of the transcendent these emotions tell us the truth. We are insufficient, the deep self-trance isn't the real "me," it's an impostor, an instrument—a useful one, but nonetheless unnecessary. These emotions are hints that there is something immeasurably more to life than what I've yet discovered or experienced.

The task, then, is not to avoid what makes me fearful, ashamed, or angry, or to entertain it, or even to act the emotions out. Both efforts, repression and expression, can lead to an emotional trap that bogs one down in the anger, shame, or fear. The task is to attend to them, acknowledge them, give them their full and rightful place in the community of the self. They are markers leading to the transcendent if we are simply attentive, nonattached to whatever happens to cross the stage of consciousness.

Attention leads to a searing and uncommon honesty about ourselves. We will not allow ourselves to be fooled. We no longer play the mind games that hid our true, real, or authentic identity. We no longer pretend to ourselves that we are unhappy or happy, deficient or sufficient, inferior or superior, helpless or victimized. We abandon all of that. We have found the foundation, the "I" behind the *I* I've mistaken for myself. Even though that "I" is not something better than what we've known up until now, the *awareness* of it is certainly better than a foggy confusion about ourselves. When we know it, we know we can never truly name it. Although we label it as a matter of convenience, it is beyond our understanding even when we are never unaware of it.

The greatest danger in any spiritual practice is that it turns into an exercise in self-meditation. How am I doing now? Boy, that was a wonderful experience! Wow, what a bummer, I hope that never happens again. Now I'm really getting the hang of it! What a fascinating insight into God: I must be really special to see it this way! We all do these and many other kinds of commentating on ourselves under the guise of spiritual awareness. My teacher, Father Willigis

Jäger, said that his job was to frustrate me. And he did a good job, just like a good golf pro who frustrates the player's swing ruts that defeat his game. The purpose of contemplation is neither to improve our morals or ethics nor to perfect our personality to win friends and influence people, nor any kind of self-improvement or self-aggrandizing goal. The "purpose" of contemplation is to lose our self: "He who saves his life loses it, while he who loses his life for my sake discovers who he really is."

It is almost impossible to do this without a ritual. Ritual makes this difficult task easier. Ritual allows us to learn how to learn. What do we learn? Nonattachment to the self-trance, the ego identity. We learn one skill, posture, breathing, breath counting, a skill that can be taught, so that we can learn another skill that can only be caught: attention, nonattachment. Contrary to the popular notion, spontaneity is the fruit of discipline, not a substitute for it.

Which bring us to Abba Macarius, one of the pioneers of Scetis, a friend of Abba Anthony the Great who was noted for his detachment and humility. Abba Macarius was a camel driver trading in niter or saltpeter, which was used as fertilizer. He died in A.D. 390 at the age of ninety. In his younger days he lived a solitary life near a village until falsely accused in a paternity case. After he was vindicated, he fled to the desert to avoid the admiration of the villagers. He once told a young aspirant who sought his advice to go to the cemetery and praise the dead. When the aspirant did as instructed, Abba Macarius told him to return to the cemetery and revile the dead. Abba Macarius then asked the aspirant whether the dead had said anything in response to his praises and scorns. "No," answered the young man. "Like the dead," Macarius continued, "take no account of either the scorn of men or their praises, and you can be saved."[2]

One day, the story says, when Abba Macarius stumbled upon a robber stealing all his belongings, he seemed ignorant of the theft. Acting like a stranger, he helped the man pack his mule and sent him on his way. This is the whole lesson of the way of nonattachment. What did Abba Macarius actually experience when he saw the thief stealing all his belongings? The story says that Macarius acted like a stranger when he came upon the robber. But it was no act. He was a stranger. He had lost his self-identity. Fundamentally, he didn't know who he was, and he didn't know to whom those things belonged. They might as well belong to this man as to anyone, and Abba Macarius might as well help him pack his stuff.

Once we get into the practice of nonattachment, which is another way of saying "letting go," all kinds of personal backlogged stuff surfaces. We let go of the comforting fiction about ourselves. We let go of the lie about ourselves, a lie we have been desperately clinging to, although we have lost awareness of our desperation and our clinging. We have become so accustomed to its troubles that we hardly experience its pain. But we shall. Shortly all the repression will surface, and we shall intimately experience all the misery just behind the fiction, for the tension that has both supported the fiction and has been caused by it is painful.

CHAPTER 5

BE WATCHFUL

Abba Ammonas came one day to eat in a place where there was a monk of evil repute. Now it happened that a woman came and entered the cell of the brother of evil reputation. The dwellers in that place, having learnt this, were troubled and gathered together to chase the brother from his cell. Knowing that Bishop Ammonas was in the place, they asked him to join them. When the brother in question learnt this, he hid the woman in a large cask. The crowd of monks came to the place. Now Abba Ammonas saw the position clearly but for the sake of God he kept the secret; he entered, seated himself on the cask and commanded the cell to be searched. Then when the monks had searched everywhere without finding the woman, Abba Ammonas said, "What is this? May God forgive you!" After praying, he made everyone go out, then taking the brother by the hand he said, "Brother, be on your guard." With these words, he withdrew.[1]

A fter the death of his wealthy parents Ammonas was forced at the age of twenty-two into a marriage arranged by his uncle. He lived with his wife until he reached age forty, and tradition has it that he persuaded her to dedicate their marriage to virginity after reading Saint Paul's admonitions. After his uncle's death and with his wife's blessing, he retreated to the desert and became a disciple of Abba Anthony. He said of himself, "I have spent fourteen years in Scetis asking God night and day to grant me victory over anger."[2] Evidently he received his wish, for he died at the age of sixty-two with a reputation for great kindness and compassion toward his fellow human beings.[3]

When we read this desert father's story with a literal eye, it appears to be a living lesson on the injunction of Jesus not to judge others: Do not judge and you will not be judged. It also appears to be a caution from a wise old man about discretion in the face of our human weaknesses. These desert fathers' stories carry meanings on many levels of our life, and we discover those meanings by engaging the story the way we engage a dream or a myth.

This story is a map for the inner journey to wholeness, or, in religious terminology, holiness. We can read this as individuals acting out a drama, which sounds plausible but misses the story's message. Each character is a facet of ourselves. Abba Ammonas, the outraged brothers, the disgraced brother, and the woman, represent the subtle interaction played out on an inner level with ourselves. This story also tells us what inner work we must undertake on this inner journey. We will first look at the circumstances from a mythic point of view to show how the mythic elements illuminate the literal situations in our lives.

The story depicts a community of monks living a well-ordered eremitical life. Each has his own cell, his own privacy. They also share a common life. They meet together on occasion for the Eucharist, and to share their work and their stories.

One of the brothers has reached a critical stage in his inner journey and is handling the situation poorly. For whatever reason, he has been thrown off balance by these new developments in himself and is trying to manage the situation by taking a lover. What man has not been tempted to resolve a personal inner turmoil with the companionship and love of a good woman? The intuition a man has at these times is correct on an inner level. It intimately involves the feminine, creative dimension of our humanity. What is breaking through the unconscious is feminine, and "she" roots us to the deepest realms of life. The anima, the great mother, the true self, Wisdom, emptiness, the Godhead, are all ways we try to describe the mysterious and unknown plenitude we call life.

Usually the male of the species is so unfamiliar with this primal reservoir of life that he bungles, looking around for it outside himself. Since he cannot see it in himself, or as himself, he sees it in the only way he can, where he can identify it and deal with it outside himself. He sees it in another, in a woman from whose womb new life erupts in pain and blood. When pristine life, which is beyond the reaches and control of the ego, begins to erupt into a man's consciousness, it is often a painful and bloody business.

The ego may instinctively try to manage the situation in an external relationship, but a flesh-and-blood woman cannot carry a man's "inner pregnancy."

As so often happens, people who are committed to do their own inner work are generally aware of what is going on in those around them. The rest of the brothers are quite familiar with the situation. But they don't know how to handle it either. Abba Ammonas visits, and they bring the case to him, asking him to accompany them in running off the brother of ill repute.

The brother gets wind of what is about to happen and hides the woman in a large cask. This is an interesting strategy. The question arises, from whom is he hiding the woman? Not from his accusers. They know and he knows they know. Nor from Abba Ammonas. Certainly the brother must realize that Abba Ammonas has been fully advised of the awkward situation. He is hiding her from himself. The large cask is only a thin disguise for the unconscious, where we hide things from ourselves. At this point in the drama, it isn't hard to imagine that the brother feels trapped in his own shame and desperate with fear.

These two emotions, shame and fear, shield us from our own tumultuous unconscious. Everyone learns early in life that shame guards what we believe is unacceptable about ourselves. But if we are to be whole, sooner or later we must summon the courage to enter the pit of shame in our backyard and deal with it, engage the demons, and pull up the hidden things about our self buried there. These discarded and unknown fragments of our self will serve us and others well when they are cleansed of our shame, redeemed from the well of our own dark side, and seen for what they are. They too have a place in us. We are incomplete and fractured until we welcome and embrace them in friendship and love. Unfortunately, as Carl Jung wrote in *Modern Man in Search of a Soul*, too often this is not the case, for a man will do anything, even die, to avoid facing himself. The folk phrase "I could have died from shame" catches well the mood of this brother of ill repute. Here, shame and death are the same. The passage leads straight ahead through his shame to death, a redemptive death, the death of the ego.

When Abba Ammonas arrives with the other brothers and surveys the situation for himself, the story says he "saw the position clearly." He takes charge without difficulty, since everyone is relying on his wisdom, and leisurely sits on a cask while the brothers try to ferret out the woman who represents the insult to their tranquillity.

The rest of the community is jealous. The other monks have promised to live a chaste and celibate life. But such promises, while superficially admirable, contain inherent and dangerous pitfalls. The danger is that promises such as these set us up for denial, for the illusion that our efforts at fulfilling the promise actually do so, when what happens is that we simply ignore a whole set of erotic energies, fooling ourselves into believing we've "conquered" what we've ignored. Our left foot may be numb, but we've still got to drag it around. Believing that this condition makes us graceful is the height of self-deception. Moralism, the assumption or belief that perfection is achievable through adherence to chosen ethical standards, is as destructive a failing as libertine behavior—or perhaps far more destructive, precisely because it looks so good. With moralism, it is the admirable quality that disguises the corrosive egotistical motives. And eventually the egotism will seep through. It expresses itself in the sense of feeling affronted by behavior that is less than ethical, in a smug superiority that disguises our inability to deal with our own unethical urges, and especially in a kind of jealousy of those who appear unfettered by ethical imperatives.

Indeed Abba Ammonas is correct in shaming the brothers for their suspicions, not because they are unfounded, but because they are misdirected. What their flawed brother has done openly, they have done secretly, and their enraged jealousy that so well masks their own erotic urges belies that fact. It isn't that their erotic urges are immoral, or forbidden, or even undesirable; it's that they are unacknowledged. By sitting on the flask, Abba Ammonas is indicating the flaw. Just as their sinful brother literally hides his sin in an actual flask, so the other brothers hide theirs in the unconscious.

We may wonder what Abba Ammonas saw so clearly that causes him to appear to conspire in a brother's immorality. The ego is threatened when life forces erupt from the unconscious, throwing our outer existence and inner orderliness into disarray. The ego feels its control slipping away, and it tries all manner of tricks to manage this fearful and fascinating event. This is a time of great danger, for the ego will try to usurp the energies and divert them for its purposes and its sense of reality. All myths warn us that the journey is fraught with perils, the passage is difficult, and one is easily turned from the inner task at hand.

There are two common strategies available to the ego to

fend off the threat. The first is to condemn the disturbing experiences and dismiss them. This is the tactic of the brothers who are set upon a confrontation. The other tactic of the ego is to seduce this creative, life-giving, pristine energy, which is what the disgraced brother is attempting.

"The position" the wise old Abba Ammonas saw clearly is precisely these two tactics. He collaborates with the brother of ill repute to keep the lid on his emerging life, hiding it not only from the other brothers but also from the brother of ill repute himself. Such a volatile experience is served poorly by those who would condemn it, and Ammonas scolds them for their condemnation, suspicions, and rancor.

But it is served no better by the brother's seduction. Abba Ammonas neither encourages the brother in his misguided affairs nor turns a blind eye to his predicament. His actions are "for the sake of God"—that is, for the sake of wholeness—a motive that will be obvious in a moment.

It is very important that Abba Ammonas takes the brother by the hand. A touch vibrates to a person's intentions and character. When the brother touches the woman, his touch is calibrated to the set purposes of his ego, his seductive strategies bent on subduing the emerging life within him and assuaging its accompanying agonies. The brother's touch is a plea for comfort and control. Abba Ammonas symbolizes the divine wholeness that is emerging in a suffering human being. A touch by this wholeness is bittersweet. Like the touch of a physician probing an injured limb, it both wounds and cures. The abba touches the brother so he can feel what is struggling to be born in him, can touch the strength and vibrancy, the boundlessness and balance, of this pristine life, the Christ life.

Then the abba, the father, says, "Brother, be on your guard." It is interesting that he doesn't tell the brother that everything will be okay or that he is forgiven for his indiscretions. We must be cautious about taking the story too literally and thus missing its message. In times of personal crisis our attention is caught up in private inner turmoil and in the urgency to find a resolution to the confusion or an escape from it. Rather than be hostage to your anguish, be attentive to the process as it is happening. Be attentive to the shame and fear, the emptiness and despondency, with which the ego greets the dawning wholeness. Take the middle course during the stormy period of transformation. Don't tamper with it. Let it happen. Let go.

Here, the story apparently ends. Abba Ammonas departs, leaving his brother to the task before him. But the abba has also left the brother with much more than practical advice for dealing with his crisis. One of the prime injunctions in the spirituality of the desert fathers is "be watchful," be attentive. The advice is so central to the mystical teachings of the desert and so easily overlooked that it deserves careful consideration.

Saint Hesychius of Sinai says of attention[4] that it is a spiritual method that, if diligently practiced over a long period of time, does three things: completely frees us from the bondage of ourselves, leads us to an intimate experience of the inapprehensible, and helps us to penetrate the divine and hidden mysteries. The work of "being watchful" progresses slowly but surely through four stages, according to Saint

Hesychius. Fidelity to the practice of attention produces inner stability, which in turn effects a natural intensification of attentiveness. Intensification of attentiveness in due measure yields contemplative insight, which in turn opens out into a condition in which a person, free from all images, enjoys complete serenity. Attention draws to consciousness an authentic, mysterious wholeness, an original innocence that is the human yearning expressed by the Garden of Eden myth. It is a reunion with the source and substance of one's being, a reunion that transforms human consciousness.

We usually notice our attentiveness when we are "paying attention to something," fascinated by the interest it arouses in us. The attention of the desert fathers is vastly more profound and freeing than the experience of focusing our powers of concentration on intriguing or chosen content. Attention is a skill we can develop and a gift we can receive that unifies the Absolute and everyday life. As a skill it means waking up to whatever flows across the field of attention, whether that is inner or outer experiences, thoughts, feelings, or perceptions. It means not picking and choosing what rises to awareness, and not hanging on to what falls away. It means not being disturbed by the content of attention, not being obsessed with it, not being compulsive about being attentive. The person who has accepted the ordeal of developing the skill of attentiveness is prepared for the gift of attention. As a gift attention means being awake and free of the need to refer the inner and outer experiences to the self. Such a one is unaware of who is attentive, free of the self and lost in God.

This is the blessing that Abba Ammonas leaves with his

brother in words and touch. Attention is the manifestation of Wholeness, of Union with God. Attention is the condition of an awakened man. Be attentive. It is a task each one of us must do for ourselves, but one for which each is unprepared. No one does it "right." Let your whole being be only attentiveness.

None of us can live a myth in our outer life. It would be a fairy-tale existence that couldn't hold up against the stress of common everyday relations. Myths are maps that show us how the energies of our inner life move, giving meaning and direction to these inner experiences. They help us take our bearings to pass through the dark and foreboding forest of personal transformation, the dark night of the soul. The path leads over the boundaries of the ego to an "unknown place," a "place" that looms up in front of us as an abyss or vast emptiness. We despair in the face of its boundlessness as we despair in the face of death. We are face to face with the primal condition of life. Letting ourselves be drawn into that is letting ourselves be drawn into an innocent, joyous freedom. There is no outside recourse now. We must summon from our self a courage we have never known before to make the passage. The myths can work for us at this inner level, but it is a tragic mistake to try to live them in our personal relationships.

Myths do not tell us how to act in the practical world or what to choose there. They prepare us for an inner freedom that allows us to choose, experience, and be absorbed in whatever happens to be happening on an outer level. Freedom makes us transparent. What happens on the outer level simultaneously happens on the inner level. The differences between outer and inner disappear, for the "I" who distinguishes them disappears. Then nothing in our life is dramatic and nothing is trivial. Life is what it is, and we are lived by *it* and not by our meanings, our purposes, our intents.

Myths and archetypes are only inner symbols for an unseen reality in the same way that icons and religious rituals are outer symbols of an unseen reality. The brothers in the story represent the ego's control tactics. The woman symbolizes the completeness of life working its way through the unconscious into consciousness. The abba is the wholeness at the completion of the journey. The story is the saga of personal transformation.

The Reality itself, however, vastly outshines the inner and outer symbols that reflect it. The myths aim us into this Reality, warning us not to be diverted from the serious task at hand. They encourage us to follow an elusive middle way that leads into a darkness we have shunned, and eventually into the Great Death and the Homecoming beyond. There are no maps or myths for the Reality beyond that threshold. We know it only by traversing the passage, attentive moment by moment.

CHAPTER 6

BECOME ALL FLAME

Abba Lot went to see Abba Joseph and said to him: Abba, as much as I am able I practice a small rule, a little fasting, some prayer and meditation, and remain quiet and as much as possible I keep my thoughts clean. What else should I do? Then the old man stood up and stretched his hands towards heaven, and his fingers became like ten torches of flame and he said to him: If you wish, you can become all flame.[1]

Little is known of abbas Joseph and Lot except that Cassian stayed with Abba Joseph for some time, and Abba Lot, a disciple of Abba Joseph, was a Coptic priest and opposed the teachings of Origen.[2] This saying is often used in a quaint way to illustrate the desirability of a Christian being on fire with love of God. While it might be read in such a fashion, it is a story with much greater depth than such a magical reading would indicate. It is a story about the transformation of consciousness, *metanoia*, beyond the capacity of the human will and faculties.

The metaphors of an amnesiac and sleep dreams can help in understanding the depth of this story. An amnesiac is perfectly healthy and functions well in the circumstances of life except that he has no memory of his own history. He does not remember his name, or that of his parents, spouse, or children, nor does he remember any other facts of his personal history.

Other people may try to reconstruct his personal history for him, but he responds to their efforts with a blank. The more he is told about the self whom he has forgotten, the more his doubt and discomfort intensify.

What he is told about himself is the truth. It is something upon which he can rely. But he cannot yet recall it for himself or about himself. He is dependent upon others to tell him what he needs to hear and cannot hear. He may even see photographs of his family and himself on various occasions with friends, but at the same time he does not "see" that person in the picture as himself.

Then perhaps one day he will run across a bit of memorabilia from the life he has long forgotten, and something will register with him. He begins to resonate with this vague and ill-defined bit of memory. It is the start of a sympathetic vibration with the reality of his forgotten life. The strings of his memory are beginning to harmonize with the facts of his history.

The purpose of a disciplined practice is to overcome the

hindrance of our forgetfulness, to awaken us from the affliction of our amnesia to the Truth of our own Original Identity. We have not only forgotten who we are, but we have also forgotten that we have forgotten, settling for the illusion of our forgetful condition. We have forgotten that we are *Deus incognito*.

This is what the Christian mystical record tells us. But it sounds so heretical, so outrageous—and frankly so crazy—that it is very hard to swallow. But wouldn't that be the reaction of an amnesiac who was picked up off skid row and told that he was actually a brilliant financier and the richest man in the world? If you lived in a world of amnesiacs and you were the only one who remembered, forgetfulness would be considered normal and remembrance crazy. This is the world of many of the Christian mystics who spoke in metaphors and parables, for a good story can slip in a profound truth before we have a chance to screen it out.

Or take the common experience of dreaming. While dreaming, we experience ourselves differently from when we are awake. This statement is obvious when we are awake, but not at all obvious when we are dreaming. In a dream we know only a timeless world of magic, shorn of memory, limited to the immediate dreamscape. Whatever happens, happens instantaneously, with nothing left over from one scene to the next. The only obvious things are the events and circumstances of the dream, which are acutely experienced at the moment.

The dream state precludes the actualities of our waking consciousness. It is not obvious to the dreamer that he is lying in bed, in a room, in a house with rain beating down on the roof. He may well hear the sound of rain but experience it as burning coals falling on his head.

Examining how we experience ourselves in a dream, we notice that we feel we are the same person as when awake, except in a dream we cannot reflect on ourselves or our experience. We can be clever or foolish, strong or weak, terrified or consoled, or whatever we are in the dream. What we cannot do is choose how we shall be. In the dream state we are the victims of the dream world, a world made in the image of our own chaotic psyches.

When the sleeper awakens, he experiences himself differently. He knows time and space. He remembers he was dreaming. He can reflect on the dream and conclude that none of it actually happened, or that it was a portent, or a revelation from God, or whatever assessment of it seems best to him.

The waking consciousness is reflective. It mediates experiences through memory, learned meanings, patterned behaviors, and preferred purposes to such a degree that we tend not to experience anything that we cannot explain or understand. What will not yield to the light of reason is either censored out of awareness, explained away, or dismissed as unreal. The world of waking consciousness is a world made in the image of our own mental processes.

When we take the dream metaphor a step further and apply it to the accounts left us by the mystics, we must conclude that the state of mind we know as waking consciousness is just a dream of a different sort, a kind of trance consciousness. Mystical consciousness is a world in which we have lost all sense of a separate self and enjoy a serenity and freedom that we can only dream about in the waking state, which is little more than a trance, according to the mystical record.

Just as the self that appears so real and vulnerable in a sleep dream disappears when we wake up in the morning, so too the self who reflects on the conundrums of life's meaning and purpose disappears in the awakening to Reality not as we think it is, but as the mystics report it to be.

That Reality is not at all obvious to one who still sleeps in the self of trance-consciousness. But then neither is rain beating on a roof to a dreamer. It is as impossible to fully understand this "hidden" Reality as it is for a dreamer to fully understand that he is "just dreaming." The point is not to comprehend mystical Reality, but to awaken to it.

Mystical consciousness is Reality. It transcends the world of waking consciousness in that it exceeds the boundaries of our thoughts and understandings. But—and this is of the utmost significance to the common misunderstanding about mysticism—it is not a world that is other than the immediate, unreflected experience of the instantaneous moment, whatever that may be. The external conditions and circumstances of life remain as they have always been. They are simply no longer interpreted by a subject who is separated from them. For there is no subject! There are only the conditions and circumstances experienced as consciousness itself. Blessed Jan Van Ruysbroeck expressed it this way: "Then only is our life a whole, when work and contemplation dwell in us side by side, and we are perfectly in both of them at once."

Reality is identical with the natural evolution of consciousness to its pristine uncluttered state, a consciousness free of the overlay of burdensome judgments on the integrity of our self and others, and limiting conclusions about the meaning of existence. Mystical Reality is not of itself mystical in the etymological meaning of that word, "hidden." It is simply obvious to one who has awakened to it. It always already is, and the awakened ones joyfully and effortlessly know that they are what always already is! Anything else is a kind of dream or trance manufactured by the human mind.

Of the many insights that modern psychology has given contemporary man, one stands out as particularly relevant to this discussion of the mystical journey. We do not live in an objective and neutral world. We live in a world charged with enchantment, which gets its power over us from our projections onto it. The shapes, forms, colors, and textures may be common to everyone, but the effects on an individual are determined by his unconscious projections on the world he experiences. Indeed, the mechanism of projection is so prevalent and powerful that it is true to say that we do not objectively experience the world. Rather, we subjectively create the world we want to experience.

To the extent that we continue to project meaning and purpose onto experiences, we are bound by limited and limiting projections. The spiritual or material quality of the projection does not matter, for it is not the quality of the projection that entraps us but the fact of projecting. And this is true whether we understand (project) the meaning of life as the opportunity to gratify our self-interest, or to adore and praise an objective redeemer and compassionate deity. For both are nothing more than subjective projections and therefore prisons of our own making. Whether the bars and walls are made of stones or diamonds is irrelevant to an inmate who is imprisoned behind them.

Our identity is entangled in our projections. Intense suffering is the price required as "the eye of the spirit" opens; that is, as consciousness expands to overtake the boundaries imposed by our projections, a suffering that we can neither appreciate nor see the purpose of, for we travel the road blindly and unknowingly. The eventual and inevitable effect of this expansion is the loss of a separate identity.

"God makes the soul realize its own nothingness" does not express the vacuity of nonexistence, but the impossibility and inaccuracy of identifying the self as anything at all. It expresses, albeit negatively, the inclusion of all that once was projected as other than the self. The "other" disappears and since there is no "other," not even the "Other" called God, to compare the self to, there is no "self." "The soul is transformed into God and becomes one and the same thing with God, just like a glass of water placed in the ocean becomes one and the same thing with the water of the ocean."[3]

The records that mystics have left are neither explanations nor justifications for their experiences. They are just facts of a Reality we find incomprehensible while we live enclosed in the projections of our reasonable and illusory world. Yet their witness to this reality, which overflows the lip of the thought that contains it, is a beacon shining back to us at the end of the way of perfection. The journey culminates even during this life in merging with the Light, being consciously "transformed into God." "My me is God," proclaimed Saint Catherine of Genoa, "…God is my being, not by simple participation but by a true transformation of my being."[4]

This is the depth in the exchange between Abba Lot and Abba Joseph. There wasn't anything wrong with Abba Lot's little rule of life, his prayers, meditations, and asceticism. Abba Joseph, however, wasn't interested in the entertainment enjoyed by a dreamer or an amnesiac. And he knew he couldn't explain the really important matter to Abba Lot. It is as impossible to explain the Reality of the Ultimate to a dreamer or an amnesiac as it is to explain to a child in the womb the realities of the "real world." Abba Joseph's response cuts through all the self-questioning and explanations right to the heart of the matter: Why not become all flame?

In almost any generation we can open the historical record and see the beacon shining out at us. Mary Magdalene di Pazzi, an energetic mystic who exhorted the pope and his cardinals, reports her experience during the ritual of the Mass, a ritual we may recall that was rich in transcendent symbolism. "I reflected upon the great union of the soul with God through the sacrament and…I felt wholly united with God, changed into God…I was with Him and knew nothing of myself. I only saw that I was in God, but I did not see myself—only God."[5] Her experience began with object—meditation: "I reflected upon…" then switched to contemplation: "I felt wholly united with God…" and ended in union: "I only saw that I was in God, but I did not see myself—only God." In this case even the medium of the sacrament that so compassionately carried human projections of a loving God, at least for past Catholics, fell away in the Reality of the Obvious, "only God."

This record is especially timely in an age when Western religions are experiencing an erosion of their moral authority and Western culture and values are cracking under the stress and strain of unprecedented social and psychological change. So many Westerners have abandoned the religious tradition of their childhoods, not so much out of spite, but because they have found no resonating challenge for their own humanity. They turn to the East for a religious message that the West has all but forgotten: God is not other than I, but is not the "I" I think I am, a truth that is realized through exacting disciplines that strip away all vestiges of an identity as a separate self.

The religious mysteries that have both inspired previous generations and symbolized for them life as it really is, not as it appears to be, seem to be fast fading. The great myths, those engines of human creativity and transcendent purpose, have been picked apart in this age of rationalism and left to wither under the scorching sun of technological realism.

There is no doubt that the leftover impoverished religious practices have not stemmed the tide of immorality that is the scourge of the twentieth century. Wars and justifications for wars continue to be the norms for behavior, not the exceptions. It is an insane world when the threat of nuclear annihilation is considered the benign guardian of freedom. The imbalance of wealth between developed and undeveloped nations each year grows wider, more embarrassing, and harder to justify. Exploitation, rationalized as virtue, wears away the dignity of human labor. The very earth we live on is allergic to our technologies. It is a what-you-see-is-what-you-get world, and for the powerful the emphasis is on "get"; the residue is for the weak to pick over.

Indeed, the problems and crises that face the human race are so complex and severe that one wonders how the human mind can work a way out of them. Read the proffered solutions. They are generally mixtures of half magic and half delusion based on an unshakable faith in deified technology. They promise to erase the evils but cost us nothing. It is truly a situation that cries out for divine intervention. Not the deus ex machina kind but the mystical kind.

One can only wonder what the shape of the world would be were it guided by the steady hand and humanitarian vision of the mystics instead of the aloof machinery of the state, indifferent bureaucracies and invisible entrepreneurs. Yes, the situation cries out for the divine intervention of the mystics: skilled mystics who know how to sensibly employ the inventions of technology, how to administer less by law and right and more by wisdom, who can point out the obvious common sense of "enough," whose visions will inspire us to abandon our hungers for more and more and yet more still. Even mystics who do nothing stand witness against human stupidity and greed.

Those who are awake are in a much better position to see clearly how to clean up the mess than are the dreamers. Mystics have no magic solutions for the predicaments of collective human madness. Even if they did, who would believe them? If a mystic told us to repent and a technocrat told us to form a committee, which one is likely to be heard in this age? As Abba Anthony the Great has said, "The time is coming when people will be insane, and when they see someone who is not insane, they will attack that person saying: You are insane because you are not like us."[6]

It is a transformation of consciousness, a remembering, an awakening, a *metanoia*, that is required now, because the origin of the present global dilemma is the dream of trance consciousness. We could do worse than to heed the wisdom of C. G. Jung, who observed that society will never be renewed until the individual is renewed, for society is nothing more than a collection of individuals. The point being: We cannot hope to resolve the dilemmas of a nightmare before we first awaken from it.

CHAPTER 7

——

SELL EVERYTHING AND GIVE TO THE POOR

Abba Evagrius said that there was a brother, called Serapion, who didn't own anything except the Gospel, and this he sold to feed the poor. And he said these words, which are worth remembering: I have even sold the very word which commanded me: Sell everything, and give to the poor.[1]

The brother called Serapion was almost certainly the learned man of the same name who had been the head of the catechetical school in Alexandria around 370 and who gave up his post to retire to the desert, where he became a close friend of Abba Anthony. He was eventually the bishop of Thumis in Lower Egypt, subsequently was

banished by the emperor Constantius, and died in exile.[2]
The saying that has come down to us through Evagrius,
who was in Egypt around the same time as Serapion, is
remarkable for a man who wrote learned treatises, one of
which, *Euchologium*, has survived. Why would a scholar
give up his books? Why leave Alexandria, the cultural center of the Roman empire, with its remarkable library, for a
desert? Why renounce the very source of his learning?
Maybe because learning and thinking and ideas don't do
much to change a person.

Our cultural prejudice favors thoughts. We place good
and "deep" thinkers on a throne and tend to worship the
cleverness of their ideas. But thoughts are weak, wimpy
things. They appear strong and bright only in the confines
of the mind. They have no life of their own. Take them out
of the mental greenhouse, and they wilt in the sun. For
thoughts to have any effect most of the time, they must be
translated from the mental to the verbal dimension. Then
what seemed so smooth and significant in the mind sounds
so contrived and thin when cloaked in words. Thoughts,
after all, are powerless. Not only are they confined to the
landscape of the mind, but they don't even stay there very
long.

Writing a book or an article or anything is an example
of that. No sooner has one started off with a central theme
than a thousand associations crowd the mind's narrow confines. One central theme turns into a magnet, indiscrimi-
nately pulling in all sorts of mental junk. Then we are put
to the task of sifting through these rusted memories to find
the useful ones in constructing what hopefully will be an

artistic presentation. When a few promising-looking bits and pieces stand out, we jot down a few notes, hoping they will metamorphose into a full-blown presentation. Later, when read aloud, they sound like the haphazard junk they are, lacking a unified theme, only dangling tangents lead off in a hundred different directions. This big mental vacuum cleaner sucking in insights and clever connections turns out to be a dustbin when the bag is emptied on the floor.

Even in their natural habitat, the mind, thoughts are weak and wimpy. They are like lightning bugs in June, flashing on and off in an instant, not shining long enough to tell what they are or to be able to locate them in relation to other thoughts.

To have any substance at all, they need the power of emotions. Take angry thoughts, for example. They are like a big fat blob of flesh sitting on a couch saying, "Feed me, feed me." When we're angry at somebody, all the little incidents that don't amount to a hill of beans get blown out of proportion like a soufflé and stuffed into a gaping mouth. And our anger gets hungrier and hungrier, and bigger and bigger, until it fills our whole mental stage and we can't think of anything else except what that son of a bitch did.

Just to show you how weak and wimpy thoughts are, even when inflated with emotions, think of a time when you ran across a person who had pumped up your anger beyond any reasonableness, and that person unexpectedly complimented you, invited you to lunch, or showed you a kindness. Most likely your bloated anger deflated faster than a pin-popped balloon.

Or take lustful thoughts. Their breeding ground is boredom and the crowd of responsibilities that weigh upon us. Pretty soon, out of this compost pile, a little flower of a thought grows up and quickly buds into a pretty romantic lover. This bloom is not well formed yet, so we ransack our memory (and we don't have to put too much effort into it), and come up with an ideal: a fine shape and subtle skin tone, inviting eyes, attractive smells, soft touches, and silky hair. Here, dancing in your mind, is the ideal lover, and you're completely under the spell. And that is all you can or want to think about. Then you get home, the spouse is upset (it's been a bad day), not all the work is finished, you're having Kentucky Fried Chicken again, the kids are ornery, and your spouse isn't even a distant relative of the illusory ideal lover. Your fantasy is dusted with the insecticide of reality, and the blossom quickly wilts. No matter how much you try to cultivate and save it, it either dies an inglorious death or you wonder how you ever could have loved this person.

At other times we don't want to be bothered by any thought. Then along comes a mental nuisance, ordinarily just a vagabond blended into the busy landscape of the mind, knocking at the door. It gains entry, of course, since we are used to entertaining stray thoughts. But it turns out to be a major annoyance. It drags along all of its numerous relatives. Before we know it, our awareness is invaded by a gaggle of thoughts, which, like unwanted, insensitive houseguests, take up residence, refusing to leave.

Thoughts are haphazard occurrences that arbitrarily change character and color. But mostly they are weak and powerless events at the mercy of circumstances. Get a pounding headache or the flu, and you can't think right. In fact, you can hardly think at all.

During meditation or times of musing, we think of God and try to make the thought stick. Or we grapple with the thoughts we have of God, hoping to exchange them for more congenial ones. Or if we can't do anything with them, we just put them on a shelf someplace in the back of our mind to gather dust over the years. Occasionally we may look at these mementos, but mostly they enjoy our benign neglect.

We try to figure God out, subjecting the Divine to the quality of our thinking. There is nothing wrong with this, of course. Just realize what is happening. We believe in God-thoughts, not God-Reality. Then God becomes the servant of thoughts, as weak, wimpy, fleeting, and compulsive as our best thinking can be.

We need to examine carefully this human act of thinking about God. Thoughts about God are cut from the same cloth as clay idols of pagan worship. An idol is a projection into material form of an alienated human weakness. And thoughts about God, to the extent that we worship them, are mental idols fashioned from mind-stuff.

Idols, whether made of clay or thoughts, tell nothing about God. They reflect the experience we have of ourselves. If God is conceived of as a stern judge, then we see ourselves as irresponsible children. If God is conceived of as a forgiving, empathetic father, then we see ourselves fundamentally immoral, sinful, and weak. If God is conceived of as the lover who loves unconditionally, then we see ourselves as unlovable and unworthy of attention or acknowledgment. God-thoughts are only projections of our experienced weaknesses, reversed and dressed up perhaps, but nonetheless ours.

Thinking doesn't reveal God: It reveals human thinking. It is a wonderful thing, thinking. But it is not God, and it would be idolatry to think that it is. At best all that thinking can do is give clues to God, the Ultimate Reality. Thoughts and ideas and elaborate mental constructs are like maps of reality, and it is important to have accurate maps. The value of a map is in both what is in it and what is left out of it, for maps are abstractions that emphasize the main features while ignoring the insignificant ones. But maps aren't reality. For a map to reflect reality perfectly, it would have to duplicate every detail down to the tiniest and most fleeting subatomic particle, which of course makes the map useless as a map. Doctrine, the religious teaching affirmed by generations of believers, is a map too—useful, but not a place to pitch a tent. It might be better to compare it to powdered milk, mostly useless, albeit valuable, until it is reconstituted with water. So mental religious or spiritual representations, like powdered milk, need to be reconstituted with personal experience.

All of which leads to one of the consistent assertions of the great mystics: God is unknown and unknowable by the human mind. Listen to Saint Thomas Aquinas:

> So when we proceed toward God by the way of removal, we first deny of him corporeal things; second even intellectual things as they are found in creatures such as goodness and wisdom, there then remains in our intellects only that he is and noth-

ing further, whence there is a certain confusion about his existence. But finally, we even remove from him this being itself as it is in creatures, and then he remains in the darkness of unknowing, and in accord with such unknowing as it pertains to the wayfarer, we are as Dionysius says, best joined to God; and this is the darkness in which God is said to dwell.[3]

Saint Thomas was referring, of course, to Pseudo-Dionysius, the unknown master of apophatic spirituality[4] who lived in the fifth or sixth century and whose writings are the foundation of Christian mysticism. After affirming and explaining the nature of God in *The Divine Names*, he follows that work up with his *Mystical Theology*. There, he negates everything that can be affirmed of the Divine:

The Cause of all is above all and is not inexistent, lifeless, speechless, mindless. It is not a material body, and hence has neither shape nor form, quality, quantity, or weight. It is not in any place and can neither be seen nor be touched. It is neither perceived nor is it perceptible. It suffers neither disorder nor disturbance and is overwhelmed by no earthly passion. It is not powerless and subject to the disturbances caused by sense perception. It endures no deprivation of life. It passes through no change, decay, division, loss, no ebb and flow, nothing of which the senses may be aware. None of all this can either be identified with it nor attributed to it...It is not soul or mind, nor does it possess imagination, conviction, speech, or understanding. Nor is it speech per se, understanding per se. It cannot be spoken of and it cannot be grasped by understanding. It is not number or order, greatness or smallness, equality or inequality, similarity or dissimilarity. It is not immovable, moving or at rest. It has no power, it is not power nor is it light. It does not live nor is it life. It is not a substance, nor is it eternity or time. It cannot be grasped by the understanding since it is neither knowledge nor truth. It is not kingship. It is not wisdom. It is neither one nor oneness, divinity nor goodness. Nor is it a spirit, in the sense in which we understand that term. It is not sonship or fatherhood and it is nothing known to us or to any other being. It falls neither within the predicate of nonbeing nor of being. Existing beings do not know it as it actually is and it does not know them as they are. There is no speaking of it, nor name nor knowledge of it. Darkness and light, error and truth—it is none of these. It is beyond assertion and denial. We make assertions and denials of what is next to it, but never of it, for it is both beyond every assertion, being the perfect and unique cause of all things, and, by virtue of its preeminently simple and absolute nature, free of every limitation, beyond every limitation; it is also beyond every denial.[5]

The truth of the matter, according to Pseudo-Dionysius, is that God is not only the denial of everything that can be fairly affirmed of the Divine, but is also the denial of the denial. The scientist J. B. S. Haldane came very close to the understanding of Pseudo-Dionysius when he commented on the discoveries of quantum physics: The universe is not only stranger than we think, it's stranger than we *can* think.

If the mind, with its human thoughts and ideas and understandings of God, doesn't reveal but contaminates the Divine, then what is a person to do to achieve union with God? Fortunately the mystics not only warn us of the dead-end streets on the spiritual journey, they have also traveled the path into the "darkness in which God is said to dwell," reporting back their experiences along the way, and most important, reporting what was beyond all experience, a kind of "knowledge" that can only be described as "unknowing." Pseudo-Dionysius compares the experience to that of a sculptor:

> If only we lacked sight and knowledge so as to see, so as to know, unseeing and unknowing, that which lies beyond all vision and knowledge...We would be like sculptors who set out to carve a statue. They remove every obstacle to the pure view of the hidden image, and simply by this act of clearing aside they show up the beauty which is hidden.[6]

"The beauty which is hidden," of course, is not external to or outside of the spiritual seeker. There is no such a thing as "objective" knowledge, or beauty, in the sense of some independent body of principles floating around the lower atmosphere waiting to be captured by the clever and the wise. All knowledge is subjective, but that doesn't mean it is invented out of fantasy. What is commonly called "objective" knowledge should more accurately be described as "intersubjective" knowledge, that is, understandings that individuals, even across cultures and across time, concur in and share.

The point that Pseudo-Dionysius makes is that the artistic medium is not something outside ourselves, like a block of marble is to a sculptor. The artistic medium *is* ourselves, and the clearing aside must be a clearing aside of our thoughts, ideas, images, and even of ourselves, to uncover the beauty that is hidden.

Saint John of the Cross describes perfectly what this is like, indeed what it is. After an experience in contemplation that was clearly beyond any capacity he possessed, he penned this poem:

> I entered into unknowing yet when I saw
>   myself there
>   without knowing where I was I understood
>   great things;
> I shall not say what I felt for I remained
>   in unknowing.
> That perfect knowledge was of peace and holiness
>   held at no remove in profound solitude;
>   it was something so secret that I was left
>   stammering.
> I was so whelmed, so absorbed and withdrawn,
>   that my senses were left deprived
>   of all their sensing,
>   and my spirit was given an understanding
>   while not understanding.

When you truly arrive there you cut free
    from yourself;
  all that you knew before now seems worthless,
  and your knowledge so soars that you are
    left in unknowing.
The higher you ascend the less you understand,
  because the cloud is dark which lit up
    the night;
  whoever knows this remains
    always in unknowing.
This knowing which is unknowing
    is so overwhelming
  that wise men disputing can never
    overthrow it,
  for their knowledge does not reach
  to the understanding of not understanding.
All this supreme knowledge is so exalted
  that no power of learning can grasp it;
  one who masters oneself will,
    with knowing in unknowing,
  always be transcending.
And if you should want to hear;
  this highest knowledge lies
  in the loftiest sense of the essence of God;
  this is a work of his mercy, to leave one
  without understanding transcending
  all knowledge.[7]

Too often in this overly busy modern world, we are oblivious to the gaggle of thoughts stuffed in the mind space. That is, we are oblivious until we try to be quiet, until we turn our attention away from the confusing business of modern living. Then we are likely to feel conflicted and

driven by mental activity stuck in overdrive. But if we persist in our effort to become quiet, eventually in due time,
our thoughts will straighten themselves out and will seem
like clouds passing across an empty sky. And, as with clouds,
we will not know where they come from or where they go
to. If we pay close attention, we'll notice that there are something like "blanks" between thoughts—tiny cracks, perhaps,
a kind of "space of no-thought." If, as mentioned in Chapter 1, something of ourselves has slipped in between the
cracks of our well-crafted self-definitions, then the place to
look for what is lost is between the cracks, in the space of
no-thought, in the place where Pseudo-Dionysius says the
hidden beauty lies and Saint John of the Cross says lies the
loftiest sense of the essence of God.

And so Serapion, the wise teacher and learned scholar,
reports—almost as a joke on himself—that he gave away
the only book he owned, the gospels, which instructed him
to sell everything and give to the poor. For Serapion discovered that what he sought in the desert wasn't in books, or
ideas, or thoughts, or some objective body of understanding. Giving away the book of gospels symbolized his giving
up himself, "clearing aside" the obstacles that stood between him and the hidden beauty. Then he discovered what
he sought, namely that he and the Beauty were not different. Both were united in unknowing, which Saint John of
the Cross says is the "loftiest sense of the essence of God."

CHAPTER 8

YOUR SOUL
IS NOT TOUGH

*Abba Sisoes the Theban said to his disciple: Tell
me what you see in me and in turn I will tell you
what I see in you. His disciple said to him: You
are good in soul, but a little harsh. The old man
said to him: You are good but your soul is not
tough.[1]*

Almost nothing is known about Abba Sisoes except for the sayings attributed to him in the
Latin and Greek collections of the sayings of the desert fathers. We know that he was the disciple of Abba Or (d. 390).
He left Scetis after the death of Anthony because he claimed
it was too popular. He went to Anthony's mountain and
lived alone there for seventy-two years. It was Sisoes who,
wishing to overcome sleep, hung himself over the precipice
of Petra. An angel came to take him down and ordered him

not to do that again and not to transmit such teaching to others. At his death he said, "I do not think I have even made a beginning yet. The angels are coming to fetch me, and I'm begging them to let me do a little penance."[2]

In this exchange between teacher and student, Abba Sisoes is the tough one in the sense of being weathered—able to withstand the elements, so to speak. The student is not so seasoned. Abba Sisoes initiates an exchange for the opportunity to point out to his student a piece of wisdom that was vital for his spiritual growth. It is often true that we cannot see our own weaknesses, and thus we don't know what questions to ask. The exchange between them is nonjudgmental. Both honestly state what they see. And both are right on target. It wouldn't be hard to imagine that together they had a good laugh over the exchange.

The story is remarkable for its clarity. Living with others on an intimate, daily basis, one often just pushes thoughts of them into the background. You get used to the idiosyncrasies, no longer paying attention to them, giving them no heed, in a rather self-protective manner. No sorting through one's irritations to check out what's on the mark and what is projection.

The disciple is breezing along, more or less satisfied to make a stab at this way of life. He is trying to save something on the side in order to save himself trouble. It is easy to go through the motions of a spiritual life. We are remarkably adaptable beings and can adjust to almost any condition in life, even the most dehumanizing. The disciple had accommodated himself to the rigors and demands of the ascetical life, but he hadn't yet developed the inner strength necessary for a complete transformation. Abba Sisoes, who did foolish things like hanging over a cliff, at least was courageous enough to be a fool. He risked. Stupid, yes! But it came from a tough soul who understood the requirements of the spiritual life: He who saves his life, loses it....

There's a difference between conditioning, training, and teaching. Conditioning is setting someone up to follow prescribed set patterns, without deviation. Much of what is labeled "education" is conditioning a person to survive in society and further its social values. In a way, it is propaganda. Training is preparing someone to learn as a farmer prepares the ground for the seed. Training is most often found in sports: cultivating talent.

Teaching is evoking something from someone in a way that isn't manipulative. To learn the lesson, one must see it personalized in another. The teacher does this by being the lesson, although it must be said that a teacher is one who doesn't think about teaching. The teacher opens himself completely to the student, lets the student see into the inner depths of his soul, doesn't hide behind a curriculum, and doesn't pretend that he is giving something other than himself to the student. What is given is elusive, for it is what is commonly referred to as wisdom. Real teaching in the spiritual life is rare—for few have trod the path all the way past the lessons and learned from their experience.

Amma Theodora said, "A teacher ought to be a stranger to love of domination, and a foreigner to vainglory, far from arrogance, neither deceived by flattery, nor blinded by gifts, nor a slave to the stomach, nor held back by anger, but rather should be patient, kind, and as far as possible humble. He ought to be self-disciplined, tolerant, diligent, and a lover of souls."

Much of what is done in this work called contemplation is training. Training the mind, the body, the self, for the time of ripening, to break through the systems and the propaganda to see things as they really are.

The anonymous author of the fourteenth-century work *The Cloud of Unknowing and The Book of Privy Counselling* knew well how austere and difficult was the journey toward union with God. It requires a tough soul to tread this mystical path. The author leads his student by measured degrees in a training in prayer that will acclimate him to the work. He doesn't mince words about what is required of the student. The student must learn to give up his thinking and his ideas about God. "I tell you that everything you dwell upon during this work becomes an obstacle to union with God."[3] And further:

> It is wrong for a person who ought to be busy with the contemplative work in the darkness of the cloud of unknowing to let ideas about God, his wonderful gifts, his kindness, or his works distract him from attentiveness to God himself. It is beside the point to say that they are good thoughts full of comfort and delight. They have, however, no place here.[4]

And again:

> Don't be surprised if your thoughts seem holy and valuable for prayer...But if you pay attention to

these ideas, they will have gained what they wanted of you...until suddenly before you know it, your mind is completely scattered.[5]

This training in nonthinking, the first steps on the journey, has a purpose: to acquire the awareness of naked being.

...go down to the deepest point of your mind and think of yourself in this simple, elemental way...do not think *what you are* but *that you are*...remember that you also possess an innate ability to know *that you are*, and that you can experience this without any special natural or acquired genius.[6]

"Your naked being" is what is left when the student strips away every attachment, every thought of God. The motive for this training is critical to the practice. Stripping oneself of everything isn't done out of contempt for possessions or other people or oneself. The motive is love of the Unknown and Unknowable. It is, in a way, raising the self to the level of the Unknown and Unknowable, for the sense of naked being is far more refined than the sense of a separate independent self with rights and possessions.

This image of naked being would later develop into the metaphor of Mystical Marriage. Just as a person strips away everything in preparation for physical lovemaking, standing naked before one's lover, so the soul strips down to the bare essentials, vulnerable and exposed before the Divine Lover. Even this isn't enough, for the sense of naked being itself must give way, resting in the being of God. In the act of making love the sense of self and the sense of other disappear, so that there is only Love without distinction. As the author says: *God is your being*.

> But now I want you to understand that although in the beginning I told you to forget everything save the blind awareness of your naked being, I intended all along to lead you eventually to the point where you would forget even this, so as to experience only the being of God. It was with an eye to this ultimate experience that I said in the beginning: *God is your being*...With perseverance in this practice, I expected you to grow increasingly refined in singleness of heart until you were ready to strip, spoil, and utterly unclothe your self-awareness of everything, even the elemental awareness of your own being, so that you might be newly clothed in the gracious stark experience of God as he is in himself.[7]

What is the training for? *God is your being* is the answer given by the author of *The Cloud of Unknowing*. Anyone who has made this journey into naked being and beyond knows how arduous and tricky it is. Perhaps this is the reason the parable of the two sons found in Luke 15:11–32 stands out more strongly for many people than much of the rest of Scripture.

The parable is a saga of transformation, a map for the journey and for the experiences along the way as one moves deeper into and then completely out of the limitations of the deep self-trance. The father represents both the beginning and the end of the journey, the source from which we arise and back to which we return, the unknown and un-knowable source. The younger son represents the way we think of ourselves before we realize who we really are. He is our delusory and limited self-identity, and everything he does is characterized by a burdensome self-consciousness, which eventually turns against him. The older son represents the deep self-trance as well, but under a different guise. He has some familiarity with the source of his being, his father, but his experiences are as yet incomplete. The deep self-trance is more subtle in him, more sophisticated than in his younger brother.

There is no hint in the parable that the father tries to dissuade his younger son from the adventure he is about to take, or correct the jealousy of his older son. His non-attachment extends to the very core of his own being, to his own flesh and blood. The story simply says, "So he divided his estate between them."

Nor is there any hint on the father's part of dependency on his sons—dependency in the sense of needing his off-spring to do, or act, or be, in a certain way for his own personal worth and value. This freedom is visible in the way the father responds to the situations that arise without warning. The younger son asks for his inheritance and gets it. He returns from his adventures, a broken and contrite man, and immediately, without stopping to think, the father accepts him. The older son complains, and the father responds without justifying himself or blaming the older son for his jealousy and resentment.

The father's nonattachment and nondependency don't imply that he is unfeeling or unmoved by the experiences of his sons. He displays a highly mature compassion toward his sons. Throughout the parable he acts immediately on behalf of his sons without evaluating the cost to himself. Compassion is more than just sympathy and empathy. It is acting on behalf of others in a wise and gentle manner.

That father is the embodiment of what the beatitudes call "purity of heart," which gives him a clarity to see things just as they are. Nothing is hidden from him, nothing is secret, nothing is obtuse. This is demonstrated in the parable when he says, "But while he was still a long way off, his father saw him...." In one sense, the younger son never left the father, for even distance couldn't obscure his presence.

The source of this "thing" I call myself, the groundless ground of my being, is manifested in this kind of nonattachment, nondependency, compassion, and purity of heart. The Unknown and Unknowable, which has no identity, is like the ocean to the wave of our individuality. And if the source is the ocean, then the younger son is a wave upon it. The wave might think itself independent of the ocean, but that is delusory thinking.

The first task of the younger son is to make a place for himself in the world, a place that is independent of his father. He must establish a healthy ego, but that also brings a sense of isolation. The ego is fundamentally insecure and turns to greediness and quick friends to mask its sense of alienation. No matter what the younger son has, he wants more. He isn't satisfied with having everything, as his father tells him, he wants to possess it all exclusively, in order to build up his sense of self.

Suffering is the natural effect of greedy independence, but it isn't an undesirable suffering. After the younger son has spent the paltry "wealth" of his ego achievements and enjoyed the pleasures of independence, he is faced with the residue, the ash, so to speak, of his illusory sense of a separate self. Suffering, like physical pain, indicates a pathology, and in this case it is ego-neurosis.

The older son also suffers from ego-neurosis, the deep self-trance, but with a difference. His trance is more subtle, lying back in the shadows. He lives close to the father yet hasn't completely lost himself in the father. He has awakened to the source of his being but maintains a separate identity. This manifests itself through a life of duty. The older son consistently did what his father wanted, but his attitude toward his duty was one of winning the approval and rewards that he supposed his father would give him. The sense of a separate self sees the source as a redeemer who will save its independence from extinction, but it doesn't yet realize that the source is the such-ness of life itself.

This leads to arrogance. The older son sees himself as better than his younger brother. He hasn't been foolish or a profligate. He isn't like his brother who has squandered his fortune and now returns broken and defeated by his own folly to escape his misery. In this respect the older brother is correct in his perceptions. But he misses the point. Both brothers attempt to establish and preserve an independence from the father. The rub is not *how* they do this, each in his own way, but *that* they do it.

The anger and stubbornness of the older brother toward his younger brother is an expression of his feeling of threat at the return and reception his brother receives. It has exposed the illusion he lives in, the illusion that duty will win for him the rewards and approval he desires. Ego-neurosis is taking the achievement of a healthy ego as the final or highest attainment possible in life. A healthy ego is a stage of development that humans must transcend if they are to avoid ego-neurosis. There is nothing special or unique about a healthy ego, no matter how balanced it is. The uniqueness is in the source.

The parable itself is a saga of transformation. We come out of God, the source of our being, the groundless ground of existence, and return to be absorbed into God, so that there is only "all in all," as Saint Paul puts it. The journey begins with seeking an independent identity, in whatever way this is done. The younger son sought his identity in the good life; his other brother in the dutiful life.

Along the way, we experience the joys and sorrows of independence, until we are finally brought to our knees in a kind of inner bankruptcy. When we reach the outward bound point of the journey, the point of a healthy ego identity, we also reach the point of diminishing returns on our accomplishments. This is a time of crisis, which came upon the younger son when a famine broke out in the land and all his friends abandoned him. Isolated and despised, he got a job tending a herd of swine. The crisis for the older son comes when his brother returns and receives a warm and grateful welcome from their father, which causes him to react with bitterness and resentment, giving the lie to all of his dutifulness. Both undergo a conversion of heart, enabling them to receive the embrace and love their father has always had for them. If we could plot this saga of transformation, the graph would look like a boomerang's path.

Conversion alone isn't sufficient, however. The final step is to be absorbed into the love of the father, for the individual wave to realize that it is one and the same thing as the water of the ocean, to be transformed in God. The father is the source of life for the two sons. Everything they have, they have from him and of him. The younger son establishes his own independence only to discover that it is an illusion. He returns to the father, contrite and repentant, and is transformed by being reabsorbed in the father's embrace, illustrated when his father gives him the best robe, the ring, and the fatted calf.

The older son also is transformed after his conversion, when his father explains to him that everything he has is also the older son's. He had no separate identity from his father, and trying to earn his rewards caused him to miss the true riches that were already his. The celebration at the end of the story is the final transformation where all are one, the younger son, his older brother, his father, the household servants, the friend—just one celebration of the Unknown and Unknowable Source.

This is more than a charming and heartwarming story of family unity as a metaphor for divine forgiveness and blessings heaped upon the repentance of a sinner. It is the story of the toughening of the soul, in the words of Abba Sisoes, to bear the burden of our rightful inheritance.

CHAPTER 9

ALL EYE

Abba Bessarion, at the point of death, said, "The monk ought to be as the Cherubim and the Seraphim: all eye."[1]

Abba Bessarion, a native of Egypt and a disciple first of Saint Anthony and then of Saint Macarius, lived during the fourth century. Doulas, his disciple, says he preferred the open air to the hermit's cell, living like a vagabond. "His life was more like that of a bird, or a fish, or an animal of the earth passing all the time of his life without trouble or disquiet."[2]

As any police investigator knows, eyewitness reports are notoriously unreliable. We see life partially at best, and often enough mistakenly. Given the same situation, one person will swear to details of an event that three others will swear, with equal conviction, are illusory. The deep self-trance constricts our vision to preferred patterns of perception, a security matrix that blunts or masks the uncomfortable edge of our anxiety over the unknown. In other words, we see what we *want* to see, what we have been *taught* to see, what we are *told* to see, what we *expect* to see. We *construct* our world, extracting from the scene before us that which we prefer and leaving aside whatever is at odds with our preferences.

Abba Bessarion is obviously not talking about the field of vision proper to physical sight, or about the registration of stimuli in the brain, or even about overcoming prejudice and preconceptions, although all of these would be included in his advice. He is talking about a quality of consciousness that can only be called complete, total, and whole. Perhaps we can get a sense of Abba Bessarion's teaching from the following anonymous report:

> As I was awakening in the morning, while still partially asleep, the scene before my eyes melted away into the real scene, as if what I'd been seeing my whole life was a colored sketch that was in every way animated, but artificial, painted over the real trees and the real sky and the real forest animals— a sanitized cartoon, so to speak. As the real scene bled through the cartoon the full weight of the reality was immediately apparent, the confusion of the unknown, the chaos of the raw sensory experience, the primitive fear of the new, the disorientation and the attractiveness of an alien place that was strangely familiar.

As Abba Bessarion lay dying, he summarized all that he learned in his years of solitary wandering in the desert: We should become all eye. Uncommon advice that sounds deceptively simple. Usually our attention is at least distracted and often diverted from what is available to consciousness. Humans are all chopped up, anticipating what happens next, consciously or otherwise assessing whether or not, and the degree to which, we are acceptable in a group, or to ourselves. He is saying that we should become completely intimate with this mystery called life, not just present, not even knowledgeable, but intimate: no blind spots, no censures on consciousness, no protective security.

We are intimate with life when we do not have to think about it, when we are completely absorbed in what we are doing like a child at play or a cat stalking a mouse. We are intimate when we have both forgotten ourselves and have forgotten we have forgotten—that is, when we are simply unselfconscious awareness. We are intimate with life when the inside and the outside are the same, when there is no discontinuity at some fundamental level in ourselves between what we are and what we are doing, when consciousness is not held hostage to compulsive self-referencing, when there are no real distinctions between what I think of as "me" and "everything else."

Only when consciousness is released from the insulation of the deep self-trance can we become intimate with life. Such an intimacy is far more radical than what we understand in relationships with friends and lovers and lacks the personal comfort that the ambience of a relationship creates. We are intimate with life when life's own terms are sufficient for us, when status, wealth, and intimacy no longer matter, when our personal security and preferences no longer intervene between us and life.

This may sound like some sort of fatalism. Indeed, without the loss of the deep self-trance, it could be a strategy for avoiding responsibility for our personal and social environment. The whole matter of freedom hinges on one point: whether or not I am in control. That is to say, whether I am strategizing to protect my sense of security or whether I have completely lost that elusive but dominant sense of self. "He who saves his life loses it, while he who loses his life for my sake discovers who he really is" (Matthew 11:39). Then we don't know who we are. We discover who we are at each instant, moment to moment. Indeed, life becomes an endless discovery, an adventure that is always a surprise, always on the brink of the unpredictable.

The period of waking up from the deep self-trance is a time of *apathia*, a phase when the emotions seem to shut down and existence becomes featureless. But it is only a temporary interval of adjustment. The emotions have been out of balance, truncated to the constrictions of the deep self-trance. They get molded to a narrow range like a root-bound potted plant. When the mold breaks, the emotions are at a loss at first, like an animal that has been penned up too long and is hesitant to pass through the open gate. Or, we can compare the deep self-trance to a closed cylinder that contains, defines, amplifies, and distorts the emotions, similar to what happens to sound in an echo chamber. So attuned are we to this cacophony that we are at a loss when the cylinder breaks open and we are freed from the echoing noise.

The emotions, even the passions, are trustworthy, for they are simply life's energy appropriately formed to the situation if they are not bound to the defense of the deep self-trance. They don't linger on, and our life becomes freely passionate, balanced, and harmonious. To say the emotions don't linger means we don't get fixated on this or that experience. When we're happy, we're fully happy—our happiness is complete in itself. So too when we are sad, angry, or frightened. Like Saint Paul, who became all things to all men, we too rejoice with those who rejoice and weep with those who weep.

It will come as no surprise that Abba Bessarion's experience as described here is not what most of us customarily relate about our lives. Most people tend to think their experiences of life are commonplace, bland, even parsimonious, when they are not caught up in the modern hectic pace of living or preoccupied with some pressing problem or other. Why are our experiences so different? Why do stories about the desert fathers and mothers, and other spiritual giants from both the Western and Eastern religious traditions, seem so extraordinary and inaccessible to common folk like ourselves? Are these spiritual heroes fundamentally different from us in some superhuman way?

Recent investigations into the nature and character of consciousness may help in answering these questions and in putting to rest a kind of infectious spiritual inferiority complex.[3] What the word "consciousness" refers to is not as one-dimensional a reality as we assume. The leading-edge studies describe multidimensional planes, or levels, of consciousness, each broader and more inclusive than the previous one.

Human consciousness has the potential to evolve through

seven or eight stages. The early stages are the archaic, magical, mythic, and rational. These are succeeded by the three or four transpersonal planes: psychic, subtle, and causal, culminating in the nondual, which is not a level so much as an all-inclusive "nonstage." Archaic consciousness, *homo impetus*, is primitive and instinctual, so much embedded in biological reality that it doesn't distinguish between itself and its environment. Magical consciousness, *homo magicus,* includes archaic but is a higher development, seeing the environment as separate from self but charged with magical figures over which it has magical power. Mythic consciousness, *homo mythicus*, includes archaic and magical, but goes a step further, ruled by the prototypal unconscious. Rational consciousness, *homo rationalis*, includes all that preceded it and transcends them in the ability to analyze its environment (social and ecological), separate out the common or social from the personal, test its results, and take on responsibility for its individuality. The next three or four transpersonal levels are what has traditionally been referred to as mysticism, which we will deal with in a moment.

Each level or rank of consciousness has a *pre* and a *trans* aspect to it. *Homo magicus* is a transarchaic consciousness, but a premythic one. *Homo mythicus* is both a transarchaic and transmagical consciousness but a prerational one. *Homo rationalis* is a transarchaic, transmagical, and transmythic consciousness, but a premystical one; and so on through the rankings of consciousness. And furthermore, each rank or level of consciousness possesses all the ranks above it *in potentia*. In other words, *homo impetus* is potentially *homo magicus, homo mythicus, homo rationalis,* and on up the line, much as a zygote is potentially a fetus, a baby, a child, an adolescent, a young adult, and so forth. To call this an evolution of consciousness doesn't mean that we humans are just monkeys with brains. Consciousness is not a particular *kind* of awareness, which would be to identify it with a particular level or rank. Consciousness is a fluid awareness in transit through higher and higher ranks until it reaches the groundless ground, the origin and source of all the lower levels that constrict and limit it.

The evolution of consciousness isn't as clear cut an affair as the descriptions of it make it out to be. There is a lot of overlapping, so that an individual evolving out of mythic consciousness through the rational stage into the transpersonal realms will experience elements of all three levels. So, we could equally talk about a mythic-rational and a rational-psychic consciousness. A cultural or social consciousness will also have a foot in all three camps, so to speak, which is the case in the developed Western nations, with the momentum pulling them out of the rational into the transpersonal realms.

Of course, it isn't very comfortable feeling the cultural and spiritual ground shifting beneath one's feet. It is far easier to hang on to a false security that denying the transitional character of consciousness offers than it is to embrace the impermanence implied in the evolutionary potential of consciousness. It is not only those who are invested in a well-established religious culture who wish this impermanent quality would go away. As an example, one of the radical discoveries of the twentieth century, quantum mechanics, used scientific methods to produce results that were not strictly "rational." The experiments that eventually led to the development of quantum physics were yielding consistent but "crazy" results. The only viable explanation was a *trans*rational one. Some unknown dynamic woven into the minutiae of matter exceeded human understanding. This revolutionary insight shocked rational consciousness, just as the previous discoveries of rational consciousness shocked mythic consciousness, and so forth down the line. Even today, a few physicists deny the validity of quantum mechanics. And they are not the exception in their opposition to something higher than human rationality. We all carry deep within our psychic structure a resistance to the transitional character of consciousness, a resistance that is evidence of the deep self-trance at work.

We are so prejudiced in favor of the dominant rational level of consciousness that we are oblivious to the fact that it is just a stage in the growth of both the human race and the life of an individual. Obviously people haven't always possessed such unquestioning faith in, or even awareness of, the benefits of science, technology, and basic reasonableness. We grew into it as a race, due to a whole host of circumstances including the advantages of a particular social milieu. Just as the present shape of the continents and contours of the land are only a phase that the earth is going through as the tectonic plates continue shifting, so too the "shape" of what we know as consciousness, its mythic-rational character, is temporary as well. Our view and experiences of consciousness and its potentials are shifting, as Joseph Campbell observed when he remarked that the problem with contemporary Americans is that they are myth-less.

One might be tempted to say that the task facing us is to rediscover, or reinvent, a mythology for a technologically advanced society. But this would be regressing in consciousness, not evolving through its transpersonal levels to finally rest in "nondual consciousness," where we are like "the Cherubim and Seraphim: all eye." Mythology is a *pre*rational story that roots people in their environment, makes sense of their lives, anchors them, and allows them to be creative and effective in their social setting. Myths work not because they make sense analytically, but because they intuitively feel right to *homo mythicus*.

Once a society, or more likely, an individual, crosses the "mythological line" into "science," it can't go back. That is, once human consciousness evolves out of mythic-rational consciousness into rational-personal consciousness, it cannot return. Evolution, in other words, is a one-way street. We evolve "forward," not "backward." Or, as the Judeo-Christian myth of the Garden of Eden has it, there is an angel bearing a sword of fire guarding the entrance to the garden. Joseph Campbell is very astute in his observation that Americans are myth-less. But he's off base when he says our task is to recover mythological consciousness. Mythic consciousness doesn't analyze the significance of myths the way we do; it lives them and doesn't even know it is doing so, because it isn't "myth" at all to *homo mythicus*. It's literally the way the world is organized and operates, which makes our accepted scientific models of reality look very odd indeed to a mythic consciousness. Rational-personal consciousness can extract the rich meanings in myths, but it can't live them because it knows that myths are only myths.

And contrary to the dire warnings and anxieties expressed by various voices, Western societies are not degenerating into a bewildering ethical haze—not, that is, any more than previous ages in transition, if history is a guide. We are not any worse off, and in many cases we are much better off, than past generations, except, of course, when we compare ourselves and our culture to the *myth* about past ages that lingers on in our collective imagination. Western societies and their citizens haven't lost their moral will. They are losing the moorings in mythic-rational and rational-personal consciousness. They are evolving *up* in the direction of Abba Bessarion's "all eye."

There is much trial and error and soul-searching in this spiritual evolutionary process, since the hand-me-down God has died. Not *the* God, but the secondhand, mythic variant has died. The *deus homini mythici* who was supposed to watch over us, guard us, protect us, and bless us here and hereafter, if we just did what was right, doesn't "work" for a lot of people any longer. Rational-personal consciousness has pretty much seen through that myth, even while it admires and savors the richer wisdom buried in it. And to modern individuals stepping ever so reluctantly into the transpersonal stages of consciousness, it *seems* as though *the* God has died, because that is the only God organized religion, ministering to a world created in the images of mythic and rational consciousness, has served up to them.

So where does one find the divine in such a lonely landscape (or mindscape) bereft of a credible deity? Especially in this age, modern man finds God where Saint Augustine said he is all the time, *a priori* to everything I can think of, and even *a priori* to thinking itself. In other words, God's not "out there" working on my behalf the way a mythic consciousness deity does; God is prior to everything that is in here, prior to my thoughts, my sense of self, my person, even to my capacity to think at all. God is not an *object* of my thoughts, devotions, or prayers. God is the *ground* out of which they, and everything else, arise, a transpersonal and transrational ground. But you can only *realize* this when you go into and through yourself, through the rational and personal, to the sphere of "all eye," the realm of nondual consciousness. The doorway to the divine is through the interior. And fortunately so, for if modern man is anything, he is a creature of interiority, a self-questioning doubt in search of a convincing answer.

This is why the primacy of individual conscience is so very vital. No one can get inside an individual to do the work necessary to discover the divine at the center or heart of everything. Even if the religion of mythic consciousness, the kind that organized religion tends to promote, tries to dictate the final truth to an individual who has already stepped past the rational-personal boundaries into the transpersonal realms of consciousness, it can't work. Because the group has no power, no real control, no sanctions, in the interior except that granted to it by the individual. A few centuries ago if you lived in Great Britain but didn't belong to the Church of England, you didn't eat. If you weren't a convinced Catholic in Spain, you got a summons from your neighborhood Inquisition representative. Religious institutions today have fewer exterior sanctions available to them to punish those who don't buy into the mythic membership religions, because Western societies, built around principles of rational consciousness, guarantee freedom of religion. Organized religion can teach, advise, and encourage the individual in his quest for the divine; but in the final analysis it must step back, trusting and respecting the individual to the point of defending the rights of primacy of the individual conscience against the onslaughts of any other claims, as Saint Alphonsus Liguori did.

The ones to teach us about spiritual maturity are the ones at the top. After all, if you try to describe a scene halfway up the ladder, *homo rationalis*, you're going to get a much different account than you would get from someone standing on the roof. The mystics are the ones who "see the whole picture." And, although the mystic reports a very different scene from what someone who is standing on the ground holding the ladder sees, the mystic at the top of the ladder is not fundamentally different from the ordinary Joe on the ground, just as an eighty-year-old isn't fundamentally different from a newborn baby—both possess all the potentials of a human being although they express them in very different ways.

And this leads to the rich mystical record buried for so long in the dusty history of Christianity. Of course, the insights need to be teased out of the anachronistic terminology. Nevertheless, mysticism is a sure map of what lies ahead of us in the evolution of consciousness. Its advice and thrust is very individualistic, which is often feared by contemporary church leaders as they attempt to salvage a communal identity. However, mysticism doesn't negate communal identity. It doesn't throw it out. It surely transcends it, but it also as surely includes it. Only the individual can enjoy "Union with God," a term for the transcendence of all personal identity in favor of the Supreme Identity, which is what Abba Bessarion's "all eye" refers to and what nondual consciousness means. The goal, if you will, of the evolution of consciousness is found in the realization that there is only One Self expressed in, and manifested through, many selves and all of creation. In one of the many paradoxes of mystical reality, this One Self doesn't absorb the individual into an amorphous glob of something or other. Rather, it is the source, substance, and expression of individual identity, meaning, and purpose. Or, to put it another way, the One Self has two faces: human and divine.

Contrary to the common misunderstanding of mystical reality, transpersonal individuation means neither solipsism nor religious narcissistic self-absorption, both of which are failed facsimiles of genuine mysticism. (This persistent misunderstanding, by the way, is, in the final analysis, an expression of contempt, an arrogance of *homo rationalis*.) Nor is it "instead of" or "in place of" mythic consciousness. It includes and assumes a cultural social/mythic identity, but it also transcends it in favor of a Supreme Identity that is boundless, and thus inclusive of all other valid, but limited, identities available and associated with the individual. Precisely because it is the Supreme Identity, it defies analysis, transcending human rational capacities. That's not negating rationality, it's transcending it.

To say that mystical reality is transrational, beyond intellectual grasp, as Saint Thomas Aquinas asserted when he said that the highest knowledge of God was to know that you don't know God, is not to say that it is trans-experiential. An ordinary human being can experience it and be transformed by it, although he can't adequately explain it or understand it. When Catherine of Genoa said, "My Me is God," and when Saint Alphonsus Liguori wrote, "The soul becomes one and the same thing as God," they were both accurately describing "something" that analytically makes no sense, that even sounds heretical to *homo mythicus-rationalis* (mythic-rational consciousness). And since the mystical record consistently affirms One Self—the soul becomes one and the same thing as God—that means there isn't "two." Since there isn't "two," there is No-Self, for "one" can only make sense in relation to "two." If "two" doesn't exist, "one" can't either. The me *behind* me is the *real me*, which ends up being *no me* at all. It is the Supreme Nothing, without which nothing is. As Saint John of the Cross has it in his schema of Mount Carmel, his image for nondual consciousness or One Self, the way to the top of the mountain is *nada, nada, nada, nada, nada, nada,* and on top of the mountain, *nada.*

The full and complete transpersonal consciousness, which is called nondual consciousness, is not another *level* of consciousness. It is the groundless ground out of which all the lower ranks of consciousness arise. It is the realization of One Self, which isn't a new and relevant myth, or a valid-in-all-circumstances ideology, or a supreme mystical experience. It is far more *real* than any of that. It is realizing, beyond story, beyond thought, even beyond experience, the source and substance, the anchor and ground, of our very existence, that which allows a person to say, "I am...," behind which there is no "behind which."

Of course, there are dangers in all of this, dangers that are more individualistic than at previous levels of consciousness. Any kind of change carries danger, and the dangers in this evolutionary process have been well explained and unmasked by great mystics like Saint John of the Cross. They basically come down to this: regressive ego inflation disguised as spiritual mastery (Jonestown and the Branch Davidians come to mind) and narcissistic self-absorption, either of the individual variant or of the group type, a snobbish and exclusive religious club.

And this is why guidance, traditionally called spiritual direction, is so very essential. Its purpose isn't to preserve the security of group membership in a religious tradition characteristic of mythic consciousness. The individual doesn't exist to serve a religious tradition: "The sabbath is made for man, man is not made for the sabbath." The religious tradition exists to serve the individual, to serve the evolution of consciousness, what we have learned as "the salvation of souls," a greatly misunderstood and misused expression. For it is what we are calling the evolution of consciousness that is salvific.

Earlier I said that each level or rank of consciousness has a *pre* and *trans* aspect to it, so that mythic consciousness includes archaic, and rational includes mythic and archaic, and so on. Another way of expressing this inclusive quality of each stage of consciousness is to say that the next level in the evolutionary scale of consciousness "saves" the previous level. The individual is saved from, or liberated from, the isolation and flaws inherent in the lower levels of consciousness. In nondual consciousness where we become like "the Cherubim and Seraphim: all eye," where "God is all in all" as Saint Paul says, the individual is saved from the narrowness and biases of mythic, rational, and even transpersonal consciousness, while the achievements of each level are preserved and redeemed. This is the meaning of Saint Clement of Alexandria's now-famous teaching on divinization: "I say, the Logos of God became man so that you may learn from man how man may become God."[4] As Saint Teresa puts it, "For it is here that the little butterfly [previous levels of consciousness] dies, and with the greatest joy, because Christ is now its life." It is here that the individual is saved from his own individuality, which, paradoxically, is returned to him multiplied a thousand, ten thousand, a million times, by all the multiplicity in creation, because *he* and his *source* are not different. If that isn't the salvation of the soul, what is? Well, at least being carted off to that happy spiritual theme park in the sky (mythic consciousness) pales to the ridiculous by comparison.

Facing the challenge presented by the evolution of consciousness means being willing to transcend a parsimonious life going in circles on the mythic-rational level. It is taking Abba Bessarion's last words to heart, "The monk ought to be as the Cherubim and the Seraphim: all eye." Abba Bessarion, the vagabond, a free spirit whom we would probably consider a bit eccentric if we had the good fortune to meet him, unlikely would have understood the elaborate schema used to explain the evolution of consciousness. Understanding or explaining the intricate dynamics of holiness is not the point. Being "all eye" is the point. The good abba had discovered the secret of the verse in Saint John's Gospel: "I have come that you might have life and have it to the full." In other words, I have come so that you may be liberated from your constricted involvement in this mystery named Life, a mystery of far greater breadth and depth, as the evolution of consciousness indicates, than the penurious existence usually referred to as "life."

CHAPTER 10

WHAT IS IT NECESSARY TO DO TO BE SAVED?

An old man was asked, "What is it necessary to do to be saved?" He was making rope, and without looking up from the work, he replied, "You are looking at it."[1]

The deep self-trance is a story we tell about ourselves, built up from bits and pieces of memory, to explain, to ourselves mainly, why we did what we did or react in the way we do, feel as we feel, or think as we think. It's a story with plots and subplots, characters, heroes, villains, and a host of minor bit parts. It gives us a sense of congruence through life's changes, an explanation for our thoughts and ideas, a *modus operandi*, a justification for all that we see we are about. We play different roles at different times in the self-story—some we play very well, others more or less so-so, and still others rather reluctantly. But it is just a story, and it always begins with "Once upon a time…"—which is to say, it is a fairy tale.

A coherent story, which includes all the major events and characteristics of our life, is a vital personal asset. The thrust of psychological therapy is to help us tell an accurate tale, not to leave anything out or to alter the fundamental facts, which are grist for the story line. For a good story gives some meaning, purpose, and use to our lives. Informal meditation is a common practice, an admirable human endeavor, an attempt to build a manageable story that we use to explain and justify our daily scenes.

The social environment and culture help, of course, because they are also stories that individuals in a group share among themselves. Society is a shared story built around the same structure and same plots as the self-story, a mirror, albeit a larger one, that reflects our inner theater. Our culture is competitive because our self-world is competitive. There are winners and losers, rewards and penalties, war and peace, ambition, cruelties, cultural biases and prejudices, and untold kindness and compassion. But these qualities are not "out there" in the dog-eat-dog world. They are reflections of the common experience of many individual self-worlds.

If we pay attention with a little bit of honesty, we'll find the evidence for this playwriting and playacting ability in ourselves. Notice how you talk to yourself, argue, beg, or correct others around you, how you set up the scenes of encounter in your mind when feeling under siege from those more powerful than yourself. Notice the period pieces that you occasionally bring out onto the stage of your memory, how you rehearse scenes, replaying them again and again until you get them "right" to your satisfaction. Be aware of these little dramas and understand them for what they are, a defense against the immediate, unreflected moment, a contraction and a limitation of yourself into a manageable scene.

This storytelling ability, the deep self-trance, gives us the illusion of a separate self, a stage manager in the wings who directs the whole play of our lives. The sense of a separate self is a false sense. It feels real, of course, because we are so entranced by our "feeling" of independence. Our belief that it is real is only an assumption that we haven't validated by our own experience. But it's just an impersonation. And like all impostors, it is very self-conscious about what it does, evaluating, measuring, assessing its performance, taking offense at rejections and criticism, glowing with self-congratulations at compliments and acceptance.

This sense of a separate and enduring self with its dramatics and story lines, this deep self-trance, is the aftermath of the tension between self-image and self-awareness. Self-image is the way we think, feel, sense, and perceive ourselves to be. In some areas we are very clear about ourselves. I like this and not that, I have this history and not another, these personality traits and moods and not other kinds of traits. In other areas we aren't as clear or as sure about ourselves. Self-image is selective and to some extent fluid, changing to accommodate new experiences and new information. A healthy self-image is always updating itself.

A weak or poor self-image tends to be rigid and unbending, dependent on outside support and affirmation.

Self-awareness is different. Whereas self-image has history, self-awareness is a-historical. Self-image is the way I see myself; self-awareness is the way I experience myself in various events of my moment-to-moment existence. When self-image and self-awareness are congruent, I sense a kind of background balance in my life. I'm not uncomfortable with the experiences that come my way, although most people are comfortable with themselves in a limited range of experiences.

Every so often, however, we are caught off guard and surprised by an experience of ourselves that doesn't fit the picture. The contradiction between experience and image causes tension that can vary from wonderment, to self-doubt, to anxiety, to terror. Managing this tension between what I think and what I want, between my idea of myself and my unruly desires, between my self-bias and my experience, creates the deep self-trance, the sense of a separate and enduring self, the story line of my life. And it's all driven by fear. The fear of falling apart.

The awareness of how fragile our sense of self is leads to a universal and potentially crippling trait: the temporality of our experiential human life. It is a given of human nature that the conditions of life are subject to change without notice. Thus, we are prone to worry. Change and worry go hand in hand. We try to prepare ourselves for the inevitable, for example, illnesses, transfers, retirement. We also habitually worry about it all, as if it's important to train ourselves to worry well.

From one perspective we seem to be composed of a bundle of worry-questions, both spoken and unspoken. These worry-questions precede us like a leash dragging us through our day-to-day existence. We are barely aware of them, so routine have they become for us, yet they start when we awaken in the morning. "What am I going to do today?" "What do I have to do?" "What am I going to wear?" "What shall I have for breakfast?" "What will people think of me if...?" "Will I be liked?" "Will I be happy?" And so many other worry-questions that set the course of our day, questions that are just beyond the periphery of our awareness, silently steering us through the real and imaginary uncertainties of life.

Our lives are incidental. We hopscotch from incident to incident, event to event, accumulating as we go a bag full of strategies and defenses for our survival, hoping that we will never be caught off guard. We have all taken the Boy Scout motto to heart: Be prepared. But when we examine our personal history, we notice that despite our best efforts, none of us has lived the life we intended. And worrying has not changed that.

Of course, bad things can happen—unfortunate misunderstandings, unexpected tragedies, and dreaded illnesses. No one is guaranteed a safe life. My life is out of my hands. It is not going to work out the way I expect or hope it will. All of my knowledge, all of my experience, and all of my planning, do not adequately prepare me to live this moment. And in some fundamental sense I do not live my life. I live an I-don't-know life. Rather, I am lived, and I am responsible for it.

The worry-questions, these anxieties, are expressions of
our egocentricity. Their parent is self-bias, the compulsive
need to preserve, at all cost, the comfortable sense we have
of ourselves. And how fragile that sense is. Change a routine, we are threatened and respond with anger, pouting, or
playing the martyr.

Wouldn't it be wonderful to be free of this theater! It
does get tedious, taking up so much of our time and energy
in posturing and dramatizing and arranging our lives into
some mildly satisfactory coherence. It is so tiresome servic-
ing the hidden agenda of the deep self-trance, which gives
everyone else their due to keep them at bay, because it expects everyone else to give it its due, independence. That's
the hidden agenda, self-preservation at all cost.

At some point in life almost everyone gets weary of
managing the tension that keeps the fiction about the self
alive. The story and strategies begin to fail, and people sus-
pect that the meanings that explain their lives, the purposes
they've dedicated it to and the use they've put it to, don't
match up with an elusive sense of life that is beginning to
trickle through to consciousness. It is time to go behind the
story to the fundamental facts of life just as they are without protective interpretations. The task is quite daunting,
for it requires the loss of self, the loss of the sense of a
personal history and a hoped-for future, the loss of everything that we've built up around ourselves. We are required
to lose the self sheathed in its protective trance.

The anonymous desert saying poses a question, but a
question that is radically different from the anxious annoy-
ances that glue self-image to self-awareness forming the deep

self-trance. It isn't an easy question to formulate, much less to ask, but it is *the* fundamental question of life. No one can help another person in this task, for all individuals must find a meaningful way of asking it for themselves. There is only one question worth asking, one worthy of an answer, one that drives the evolution of consciousness: How do I face life? In the story someone asked an old man, a hermit in the desert, the question this way: "What is it necessary to do to be saved?" Whoever this person was in the story, he or she paid an enormous price to ask this question, which was formulated out of personal experiences, doubts, and humility.

We hope that the right person, the right reputation, the right physical conditions, the right psychological experiences, will result in our contentment. We aren't looking for genuine happiness. We are looking for its counterfeit, relief and satisfaction. In other words, we believe in the "and-they-lived-happily-ever-after" syndrome. We might laugh at it on the surface, but at a deeper level no one can really convince us that it is just a fairy-tale ending. It takes years of life experience to erode our infantile faith. Again and again, we mistakenly build our hopes on the same optimistic assumptions, only to be disappointed again and again. For happiness is independent of, and prior to, any and all of life's circumstances and conditions.

Our immediate tendency is to overlook our present experience, in search of an ideal formula for happiness. We neglect to see in the current conditions and circumstances of our life the happiness we pursue under the camouflage of contentment. As a result, the unavoidable, unexpected, and unwanted fruit of our search is doubt, a doubt that, if allowed to work its magic, will focus a glaring light on our own inadequacy. We live a gray and bland existence peppered periodically with excitement. If we are prepared to learn from our experiences and to bear the burden of doubt, then we will be led to humility. Humility is the simple and keen awareness that we cannot help ourselves in any fundamental way. We cannot make ourselves happy. We cannot make ourselves good. We cannot save ourselves from our foolishness. But we might be able to learn what we can do.

An uncommon honesty was behind the question this unknown person asked: "What is it necessary to do to be saved?" It was a question that welled up from the depths of his being like a groan. It drove him to despair, but it also drove him to the desert.

Just as it is rare to ask this question, so it is rare to have it answered so clearly and compassionately. In the current religious climate those who are prepared to ask such a personally challenging question too often encounter stock religious answers with all the life drained from them. The old man's response was neither trivial nor flippant. Nor is it as simplistic as it at first sounds. The old hermit had done his work, which burned away the opaque filter of his self-bias so that he saw vividly and keenly life just as it is. One with the Divine, he was free to find himself and the Divine in whatever happens to be happening. Another anonymous desert saying has it, "God investigates three things in us: mind, word and deed."[2] This old man had penetrated to the heart of nondual consciousness, had gone past the contradiction between emptiness and mental content appreciating the rightful place of the intellect, and expressed his liberation in the everyday ordinary events and obligations of life. In a later century another anonymous spiritual master would express this liberation for one of his troubled students this way:

> Put the strict way on one side and the lax way on the other, and look instead for what is hidden between them; once you have found this you will be free in spirit to pick up or leave any of the other things as you wish...What, you may ask, is this hidden something? Quite simply, it is God...God is hidden between them, and you cannot find him with your intelligence....So choose him, and you will be silently speaking, speaking silence, eating in fasting, fasting in eating, and so forth....This loving choice of God, knowing what to set aside in order to seek him out with the steadfastness of a pure heart, being able to put both opposites aside when they present themselves as the be-all and end-all of spiritual aspirations, is the best way of finding God you can learn in this life.[3]

What is it necessary to do to be saved? The old man "was making rope and without looking up from the work, he replied, 'You are looking at it.'" It doesn't sound like a very profound answer. However, the answer fitted the question perfectly. The old man took the measure of the person before him and compassionately revealed the obvious, and the almost obvious, to this young seeker on the verge of liberation from the conflicts and fictions of an independent and separate self.

It is so tempting to set religion apart from the ordinary,

making of it a sort of fairyland amusement park. This is a modern-day rendition of an ancient heresy, Manicheism, which tried to separate reality into spirit and matter, the sacred and the profane. Salvation is healing that illusory split. How do we do that? We don't. It is already done. It already always is. The "split" between God and man, the ordinary and the holy, the sacred and the profane, is a prop in our imaginary self-story. It does not exist and never really did. Our task is to realize that fact.

Salvation is an everyday ordinary experience. If Christianity really does proclaim good news, then the good news is that everything is redeemed. Nothing is condemned. All that is left to do is to realize it. No condition of life precludes happiness. No condition of life increases it. For a given individual making rope is as holy and effective and expressive as any ritual religious act. The simple act of making rope, or washing dishes, or walking to the office, or talking on the phone, does not imply anything other than itself. Nor is it meant to. Everything is as it should be. Give up the search. It is right here. It is obvious.

CHAPTER 11

———

SEEK GOD

Abba Sisoes said: Seek God, and do not seek where he dwells.[1]

Western societies are in the throes of a revolutionary cultural transition. Many commentators on the so-called paradigm shift recognize that we are at the end of the Age of Reason. The first indicators of this transformation, it is generally acknowledged, arose in the hard sciences during the early part of this century. Quantum physics signaled the end of the mechanized-universe model developed during the Enlightenment. Reality, as represented by Newtonian physics and the other sciences, thought to be certain and inerrant, was discovered to be ambiguous and arbitrary. And the result? The stable boundaries, established by the science of the Age of Reason, shifted within a relatively short period of thirty years.

The discovery of quantum physics has had a revolutionary impact on the consciousness of the developed societies.
If one cannot depend on the ground beneath one's feet, so
to speak, and the nature of reality is itself uncertain, then
how can one depend on anything?

How did quantum physics change consciousness? When
you discover that the world, the reality you're living in, is
essentially indefinable, unknowable, and indeterminate, you
are saying that you are essentially indefinable, unknowable,
and indeterminate. We are not isolated beings. We are
"beings-in-relation." When the "what" we are related to,
namely our environment, is discovered to be ambiguous, then
the "who" that is related to it is ambiguous. This has led to
an individual quest in answer to the terribly important question "Who am I?" Quantum physics ushered in an identity
crisis that is still developing in Western consciousness.

It also brought a lot more into question. The very na-
tures of institutions are in doubt. Once the uncertainty discovered by quantum physics crept into general public awareness, the institutional flaws and faults were no longer pro-
tected from scrutiny. If science can question the rock-solid
stability and demonstrate the insubstantiality of reality, the
very anchor of human identity, then questioning anything
else is anticlimactic. Recently institutions in the United States
have been embarrassingly examined in very public detail.
And it is no accident that this scrutiny is instigated by individuals who claim to have been damaged by the institution
in question. Goliath is wounded by David.

Faced with an uncertainty of this magnitude, irrevoca-
bly visited upon the modern psyche, citizens in the West

have turned to the only place they know for the stability they need: themselves, or more precisely, their individuality. The twentieth century has seen an explosive growth in psychology and personal therapy, because with the dawn of quantum physics there is nothing outside of oneself that is reliable. And even *that* "self" is in doubt. If the modern person can't rely on the social structures and institutions, at least he can rely on his doubt. One thing that isn't in doubt for a modern person is doubt itself. He may be isolated and adrift in a shifting world that undercuts his sense of self, but he is not completely impotent. He may not be able to change the circumstances of his existence, but he can work with the doubt; his personal, individual doubt. He can't doubt *doubt*!

Organized religion's response to this has been tepid at best, and at its worst a condemnation of "individualism" as an aberration of the human spirit. For the modern person caught in the dilemma of cultural transition, this is a rather ambiguous and misleading response. If organized religion means by individualism "narcissistic self-absorption," then it is right to sound the alarm. But too often today we hear a condemnation of the only viable avenue available to us in an age of uncertainty, which perplexes us even more.

Organized religion's condemnation of individualism is doubly puzzling to us because we didn't choose an identity crisis. We discovered it. We aren't responsible for it. It is the milieu in which we live. The attempt to reassert the truths of faith through old religious myths and their practical expressions doesn't work for the modern individual because quantum physics not only brought doubt ("Who am I?"), it also revealed the next plane of consciousness, a level of awareness that transcends mythology, religious or secular.

The "evolution of consciousness" is a phrase often used to describe what is happening in the West during this time of transition. The discoveries of quantum physics were possible not simply because we developed an external means, technology, to make the scientific observations, but *first of all* because an internal means, a type of consciousness, evolved to interpret the data correctly and to validate the interpretation. Galileo, we recall, ran into trouble not because of inadequate technology, but because too many powerful men *wouldn't* look through the telescope to *see* the data, much less try to interpret it. Our embarrassment over this incident three centuries later is evidence that we have evolved past the mythic consciousness that so hamstrung Galileo.

If the assessment is correct that Western societies have a foot in the mythic realm and a foot in the transpersonal realm, straddling rational consciousness with the momentum of the step leaning toward the transpersonal, then there are perhaps three options available to a person seeking a reliable religious reality for today.

The most talked about because of its political agenda is a subservient literalism, either of the "biblical" variety that tends to be uniquely American, named fundamentalism, or the Catholic variant, obsessive obedience to centralized church authority, bordering on the pathological, named "traditionalism." The shared characteristic of both fundamentalism and traditionalism is an abdication of personal responsibility in favor of a supposed security and certainty in an objective norm, either the Bible or Rome. In other words, the objective religious norm isn't a guide to greater personal responsibility for one's spiritual growth and maturity, which both Sacred Scripture and Church authority are meant to be, but a substitution for it. This option answers the question "Who am I?" by saying: "Don't ask!"—solving the dilemma by denying it.

The second option is a kind of abdication to "institutional realities," an attitude that tends to harbor either indifference or cynicism. Many Americans who believe in God fall into this category. They treat religion respectfully, as one facet in the makeup of a genuine American life, but consider serious spirituality arcane or esoteric. Religion is part of the social identity, but it is not a force for personal renewal and change. When individuals give religion greater attention than normal, their reflections seem to have more in the nature of intellectual curiosity than a formative focus. This is the "status quo" option, which more or less goes along with whatever contemporary religious trend the mainline churches are endorsing. This option answers the question "Who am I?" by saying: "Huh?"—solving the dilemma by ignoring it.

The third option is a kind of skepticism about organized religion in favor of spiritual growth. Eastern religions and practices such as Yoga and Zen, so called New Age philosophies and the occult, Christian mysticism, and other kinds of noninstitutional spiritual programs continue to attract Westerners who reject the literalists' mentality and who are dissatisfied with the religious status quo. These people seek a spiritual reality that they can validate through personal experience independent of, but not necessarily opposed to, the traditional religious institutions. Whatever organization they have tends to be around a recognized spiritual guide, either an accomplished master or a spiritual program, instead of religious institutional authority. This option answers the question "Who am I?" by saying: "Right question!" It doesn't solve the dilemma, but it engages it.

All three of these contemporary categories have their strengths and weaknesses. The issue is not which is better than the other two, or even which shall predominate as Western societies undergo a cultural transition. The question is: What religious or spiritual model is Western culture evolving toward?

The men and women of the desert also lived in a disorienting age of transition during the fourth century, with its accompanying unique identity crisis. The Roman empire under Constantine (A.D. 306–337) officially recognized Christianity, eventually mixing religious and secular authority and bringing to an end the age of the martyrs, those who witnessed to the gospel with their blood. The Christian culture shifted from a persecuted underground movement to a legitimate institution destined for immense influence in secular society. Those who fled to the Egyptian desert sought to live the ideals of the gospels away from what they understood as a corruption of Christianity in a corrupt society. The sayings that have come down to us in the *Verbum Seniorum* and the *Apophthegmata* are the stories and teachings of these holy men and women of the desert. These kernels of spiritual wisdom are relevant to any age, and perhaps especially to our own.

The desert Christians sought to resolve their identity crisis through living the gospel in their daily lives. Theirs was an experiential, practical understanding of the teachings of the Savior that seeped into the pores of their being and that may be summarized in this anonymous desert saying: "An old man said, 'I never wanted work which was useful to me but loss to my brother. For I have this expectation, that what helps my brother is fruitful for me.'"[2] In their sayings there is little of a detached intellectual comprehension, which too easily floats on the surface of awareness like oil on water, of the core Christian message. But there is little doubt they understood that God's essence is love and that the footprints of love of God are love of neighbor and enemy alike. They were transformed into the tripartite cardinal directive of Christianity and the goal of spiritual maturity, love God, love self, and love others. They lost themselves, for charity required nothing less of them. They understood that love is not a particular action, thought, message, or motive. Love is the effect of letting go of the self.

> A brother said to an old man, "There are two brothers. One of them stays in his cell quietly, fasting for six days at a time, and imposing on himself a good deal of discipline, and the other serves the sick. Which one of them is more acceptable to God?" The old man replied, "Even if the brother who fasts six days were to hang himself by the nose, he could not equal the one who serves the sick."[3]

A life of letting go of the self is generally a very ordinary life without drama, as the desert Christians' lives illustrate.

It is doing the ordinary things of daily living without the burdensome preoccupation of self-conscious evaluation, without the common tedious wondering whether one is right or wrong, good or bad, the tiresome guessing whether one will be accepted or rejected, loved or ignored; all the play-by-play commentating that runs through the mind. Christian perfection, charity, is simply free of the tyranny of the self.

"If I pray to God that all people might be inspired because of me, I would find myself repenting at the door of every house. I would rather pray that my heart be pure toward everybody," said Amma Sarah.

Losing the self may strike a contemporary person as odd and dangerous. It is common to point out the psychological dangers of being free of the self, dangers that are indeed very real when the loss of self is premature. But it is uncommon to point out the dangers of not being free of the self, dangers that are too easily overlooked or dismissed. Does the freedom to pursue any personal interest or desire really make us masters, in a way that makes a difference, of some small portion of the inner and outer events of our lives? Isn't that just a mirage of freedom that only seems real because our culture says it's real? Isn't it closer to the truth to say that this supposed freedom is really our fears and regrets pursuing us, our hopes and fantasies enslaving us?

We are reminded of the true nature of this supposed freedom every time we lose our tempers, are beside ourselves with fear, possessed by lust, lost in thought, preoccupied with some minor inflated concern, overcome by loneliness, obsessed by prejudice, covered with shame, or a victim of depression. We are required to slip loose from the bonds of these multiple manifestations of the self the gospel requires us to lose. They are the hidden masters of our lives, who, while wearing a disguise of freedom, pull on the short leash that ties us up.

Spiritual interests and desires are especially tricky when it comes to forgetting the self. Any thought that one is "living for God," or any sentiment that God lives in oneself, can be no more than self-righteousness and a pernicious form of it when it leads to crimes in the name of religion. (The great danger in religious self-righteousness is that the human ego replaces the Divine Reality and may even create a dehumanizing ideology to justify the violation of human dignity and rights, all in the name of God, of course.) In truth, upon careful inspection with courageous honesty, the desert Christians discover that they did not do a single thing for the love of God, and God did not live in them. God lived them! God lived them as the whole experience of the moment, and they were responsible for all of it.

The way a mystic would say it is: "I am love." He does not mean the "I" we are accustomed to, however. Not the peculiar collection of favorite thoughts and notions, the preferred patterns of mental, emotional, and physical responses that we assume composes our unique identities. Not *that* I. Rather the unknown and unknowable "I" that is behind *that* I; the "I" that is free of *that* I, is the "I" of the mystical "I am love." It is here that the mystics of the desert found themselves, in the freedom love offers.

One day Abba John was sitting down in Scetis, and the brethren came to him to ask him about their

thoughts. One of the elders said, "John, you are
like a courtesan who shows her beauty to increase
the number of her lovers." Abba John kissed him
and said, "You are quite right, Father." One of his
disciples said to him, "Do you not mind that in
your heart?" But he said, "No, I am the same inside as I am outside."[4]

The new commandment that the Savior taught, "Love
one another as I have loved you," is both a practical means
for forgetting the self and the inevitable expression of the
self forgotten. The prime injunction, love, requires under
all circumstances and conditions that the followers of the
Savior surrender whatever arises of the self. Yet the more a
person deliberately attempts to practice this kind of radical
self-forgetting, the more likely that person is to run up
against the self he is trying to forget.

However, at some point in one's fidelity to the practice,
and in an unknown manner, one quite effortlessly transcends
the barriers of self to discover what already always *is*. There
is only *that*. And in the Christian tradition the unknowable
that is called Love. Then one knows by a mysterious "unknowing" the great truth expressed in Saint John's first letter: "God is love, and those who abide in love abide in God,
and God abides in them...because as he is, so are we in this
world" (1 Jn. 4:16).

An old man was asked, "What is it necessary to do
to be saved?" And he answered, "Practice everything that is good and avoid everything that is evil."[5]

NOTES

Introduction

1. Athanasius, *The Life of St. Antony and The Letter to Marcellinus,* ed. and trans. Robert C. Gregg (Mahwah, N.J.: Paulist Press, 1980), 39.
2. Norman Russell, trans., *The Lives of the Desert Fathers, The Historia Monachorum in AEgypto.* (Kalamazoo, Mich: Cistercian Publications: USA. Kalamazoo, Mich., 1981).
3. See Benedicta Ward's Introduction to *The Lives of the Desert Fathers.* (Ibid.)
4. Russell, *The Lives of the Desert Fathers,* 101.
5. Ibid., 107.
6. *De Vitis Patrum, Liber Tertius, Verba Seniorum,* no. 104

Chapter 1

1. T. Merton, 1970. *The Wisdom of the Desert* (New York: New Directions, 1970), 30.
2. Jacob Needleman, *Consciousness & Tradition* (New York: Crossroad, 1982), 81.

Chapter 2

1. B. Ward, tr., *The Sayings of the Desert Fathers*. (Kalamazoo, Mich.: Cistercian Publications, 1975), 102.
2. *Butler's Lives of the Saints*. (New York: P. J. Kenedy & Sons, 1956), III, 418.

Chapter 3

1. Y. Nomura, *Desert Wisdom* (Garden City, N.Y.: Image Books, 1984), 26.
2. Merton, 73–74.
3. Ward, 234.
4. J.A. Walsh, ed. and trans. *The Cloud of Unknowing* (Mahwah: N.J.: Paulist Press), 134.
5. Teresa of Avila, *The Interior Castle,* IV, 3, 19, 332.
6. Nomura, 32.
7. C. Jones, G. Wainwright, and E. Yarnold, eds. *The Study of Spirituality* (New York: Oxford University Press, 1986), 244–45.
8. Ward, 1.
9. Ward, 74.

Chapter 4

1. Nomura, 62.
2. Ward, 132.

Chapter 5

1. Ward, 28.
2. Ibid., 26.
3. *Butler's Lives of the Saints*, IV: 32–33.
4. *The Philokalia* (London: Faber & Faber), I: 162–63.

Chapter 6

1. Nomura, 90.
2. Ward, 101 and 121.
3. Saint Alphonsus Liguori, *Guide for Confessors:* from the

Praxis Confessorii, R. Schiblin, ed. (Published privately), Chapter 9.

4. Quoted in Evelyn Underhill, *Mystics of the Church* (Cambridge, England: James Clarke & Co., 1975), 165.

5. Quoted in H.A. Reinhold, ed., *The Soul Afire: Revelations of the Mystics* (Garden City, N.Y.: Image Books, 1973) 349.

6. Nomura, 15.

Chapter 7

1. Nomura, 18.

2. *Butler's Lives of the Saints*, I: 655–56.

3. Saint Thomas Aquinas, I *Sententiae,* d. 8, q. 1, a. 1., ad 4.

4. Kataphatic spirituality, from the Greek *kataphemi,* "to say yes, to assent," emphasizes the similarity between the Creator and the created, encouraging the use of positive mental images, ideas, and affections in prayer. Kataphatic spirituality is the prelude to and preparation for apophatic spirituality, from the Greek *apophemi* "to say no, to refuse." Apophatic spirituality employs imageless or objectless prayer in order to attain, through grace, to the Divine Reality that completely surpasses all human understanding, culminating in Mystical Marriage.

5. C. Luibheid, trans., *Pseudo Dionysius: The Complete Works* (Mahwah, N.J.: Paulist Press, 1987), 140–41.

6. Ibid., 138.

7. K. Kavanaugh, and O. Rodriguez, trans. *The Collected Works of St. John of the Cross* (Washington, D.C.: ICS Publications, 1964), 718–19.

Chapter 8

1. Nomura, 97.

2. Ward, 212–22.

3. William Johnston, trans. *The Cloud of Unknowing* (Garden City, N.Y.: Image Books, 1973), 54.

4. Ibid., 59.

5. Ibid., 55.

6. William Johnston, ed. and trans. *The Book of Privy Counselling*. (Garden City, N.Y.: Image Books, 1973), 152–53.
7. Ibid., 171–72.

Chapter 9

1. Ward, 42.
2. Ibid., 40–43.
3. Cf. Ken Wilber, *The Spectrum of Consciousness*, (Wheaton, Ill.: Quest Books, 1997, 1993) and *Sex, Ecology, Spirituality: The Spirit of Evolution* (Boston: Shambhala, 1995); also, Jean Gebser, *The Ever-Present Origin* (Athens, Ohio: Ohio University Press, 1985).
4. Quoted in B. McGinn, *The Foundations of Mysticism: Origins to the Fifth Century* (New York: Crossroad, 1992), 107.

Chapter 10

1. C. Stewart, OSB, trans. *Apophthegmata*, XX [91] *World of the Desert Fathers* (Fairacres, Oxford, England: SLG Press, 1986), 35.
2. Ibid., LI (122): 38.
3. *A Much-Needed Letter on Moderation*, ascribed to the author of *The Cloud of Unknowing*.

Chapter 11

1. Ward, 220.
2. Nomura, 31.
3. Ibid., 66.
4. Ward, 95–96.
5. Stewart, *Apophthegmata*, XXIV, 36.

BIBLIOGRAPHY

Armstrong, K. 1994. *A History of God*. New York: Ballantine Books.

Athanasius. 1980. *The Life of St. Antony and The Letter to Marcellinus*, ed. and trans. Robert C. Gregg. Mahwah, N.J.: Paulist Press.

Blakney, R. 1941. *Meister Eckhart*. New York: Harper & Row.

Brianchaninov, I. 1993. *On the Prayer of Jesus: From the Ascetic Essays of Bishop Ignatius Brianchaninov*. Rockport, Mass.: Element Books.

Burke, R. 1969. *Cosmic Consciousness*. New York: E.P. Dutton.

Coward, H. 1985. *Jung and Eastern Thought*. New York: SUNY Press.

De Jaegher, P., ed., and Attwater, D., trans. 1977. *An Anthology of Christian Mysticism*. Springfield, Ill.: Templegate.

Edinger, E. 1992. *Ego and Archetype: Individuation and the Religious Function of the Psyche*. Boston: Shambhala.

Enomiya-Lassalle, H. 1988. *Living in the New Consciousness*. Boston: Shambhala.

Forman, K.C. 1994. *Meister Eckhart: Mystic As Theologian*. New York: Continuum.

Fox, M. 1980. *Breakthrough: Meister Eckhart's Creation Spirituality in New Translation*. Garden City, N.Y.: Image Books.

Goleman, D. 1988. *The Meditative Mind: The Varieties of Meditative Experience*. New York: Jeremy P. Tarcher/Perigee Books.

Granfield, D. 1991. *Heightened Consciousness: The Mystical Difference*. Mahwah, N.J.: Paulist Press.

Hixon, L. 1989. *Coming Home: The Experience of Enlightenment in Sacred Traditions*. Los Angeles: Jeremy P. Tarcher.

Huxley, A. 1990. *The Perennial Philosophy*. San Bernardino, Cal.: Borgo Press.

_____. 1963. *The Doors of Perception* and *Heaven and Hell*. New York: Harper & Row.

Jäger, W. 1987. *The Way to Contemplation: Encountering God Today*. Mahwah, N.J.: Paulist Press.

_____. 1994. *Contemplation: A Christian Path*. Liguori, Mo.: Triumph.

_____. 1995. *Search for the Meaning of Life: Essays and Reflections on the Mystical Experience*. Liguori, Mo.: Triumph.

Johnston, W. *The Mysticism of the Cloud of Unknowing: A Modern Interpretation,* 2nd ed. New York: Desclée Company.

_____. ed. 1973. *The Cloud of Unknowing and the Book of Privy Counselling*. Garden City, N.Y.: Image Books.

_____. 1976. *Silent Music: The Science of Meditation*. San Francisco: Harper & Row._____. ed. 1973.

Jones, C., Wainwright G., Yarnold, E., eds. 1986. *The Study of Spirituality*. New York: Oxford University Press.

Kavanaugh, K., and Rodriguez, O., trans. 1991. *The Collected Works of St. John of the Cross*. Washington, D.C.: ICS Publications.

Liguori, St. Alphonsus. *Guide for Confessors: from the Praxis Confessarii*. Ed. R. Schiblin. Privately published, n.d.

Luibheid, C. 1987. *Pseudo Dionysius: The Complete Works*. Mahwah, N.J.: Paulist Press.

Mantzaridis, G. 1984. *The Deification of Man: St. Gregory Palamas and the Orthodox Tradition*. Crestwood, N.Y.: St. Vladimir's Seminary Press.

McGinn, B. 1994. *The Foundations of Mysticism: Origins to the Fifth Century*. New York: Crossroad.

Merton, T. 1970. *The Wisdom of the Desert*. New York: New Directions.

Needleman, J. 1982. *Consciousness and Tradition*. San Francisco: Harper & Row.

_____. 1993. *Lost Christianity: A Journey to Rediscovery to the Center of Christian Experience*. Rockport, Mass.: Element Books.

_____. 1986. *The Heart of Philosophy*. San Francisco: Harper & Row.

Nomura, Y. 1988. *Desert Wisdom: Sayings from the Desert Fathers*. Garden City, N.Y.: Image Books.

Reinhold, H.A. ed. 1973. *The Soul Afire: Revelations of the Mystics*. Garden City, N.Y.: Image Books.

Smith, H. 1992. *Forgotten Truth: The Perennial Wisdom of Religious Tradition*. San Francisco: Harper.

Stewart, C. 1986. *The World of the Desert Fathers*. Fairacres, Oxford: SLG Press.

Underhill, E. 1988. *Mystics of the Church*. (reprint pap. ed.) Ridgefield, Conn.: Morehouse Pub.

_____. 1960. *The Essentials of Mysticism*. New York: E.P. Dutton.

Walsh, J.A., trans. and ed. 1988. *The Pursuit of Wisdom and Other Works*. Mahwah, N.J.: Paulist Press.

_____. trans. 1981. *The Cloud of Unknowing*. Mahwah, N.J.: Paulist Press.

Ward, B. 1975. *The Sayings of the Desert Fathers*. Kalamazoo, Mich.: Cistercian Publications.

Washburn, M. 1987. *The Ego & the Dynamic Ground*. New York: SUNY Press.

Welch, J. 1982. *Spiritual Pilgrims: Carl Jung and Teresa of Avila*. Mahwah, N.J.: Paulist Press.

White, J., ed. 1995. *What Is Enlightenment: Exploring the Goal of the Spiritual Path*. New York: Paragon Hse.

Wilber, K. 1977. *The Spectrum of Consciousness*. Wheaton, Ill.: Quest Books.

_____. 1979. *No Boundary: Eastern and Western Approaches to Personal Growth*. Boston: Shambhala.

_____. 1983. *A Sociable God: Toward a New Understanding of Religion*. Boston: Shambhala.

_____. 1983. *Eye to Eye: The Quest for the New Paradigm*. Garden City, N.Y.: Anchor Press.

_____. 1983. *Up from Eden: A Transpersonal View of Human Evolution*. Boston: Shambhala.

_____. 1985. *The Atman Project: A Transpersonal View of Human Development*. Wheaton, Ill.: Quest Books.

_____. 1995. *Sex, Ecology, Spirituality: The Spirit of Evolution*. Boston: Shambhala.

Wolinsky, S. 1991. *Trances People Live: Healing Approaches in Quantum Psychology*. Bearsville, N.Y.: Bramble Company.

_____. 1993. *Quantum Consciousness: A Guide to Experiencing Quantum Psychology*. Bearsville, N.Y.: Bramble Company.

_____. 1994. *The Dark Side of the Inner Child: The Next Step*. Bearsville, N.Y.: Bramble Company.

Zukav, G. 1990. *The Seat of the Soul*. New York: Simon & Schuster, A Fireside Book.

ABOUT
THE AUTHOR

Gregory Mayers is a Redemptorist priest who has worked in retreat and spiritual direction ministries for more than twenty years. He is currently director of the Bishop DeFalco Retreat Center in Amarillo, Texas. Trained in the Western tradition of contemplative practice under the direction of Willigis Jäger, he is also a student of the Sambo-Kyodan school of Zen. He holds M.Div. and M.R.E. degrees from the University of the State of New York. In 1971 he founded "The Contemplative Path," an institute dedicated to the teaching and practice of contemplation and Zen. He is also a qualified "Journal Consultant" for the Dr. Ira Progoff *Intensive Journal* Workshop and gives these workshops throughout the country. This is his first book.